# NEW BEGINNING, NEW HOPE

## Words of POPE FRANCIS

### Holy Week Through Pentecost

# New Beginning, New Hope

---

## Words of POPE FRANCIS
### Holy Week Through Pentecost

---

Our Sunday Visitor Publishing Division
Our Sunday Visitor, Inc.
Huntington, Indiana 46750

Copyright © 2014 by Libreria Editrice Vaticana.

Copyright © 2014 by Our Sunday Visitor Publishing Division, Our Sunday Visitor, Inc. Published 2014.

19  18  17  16  15  14      1  2  3  4  5  6  7  8  9

ISBN 978-1-61278-767-1 (Inventory No. T1573)
eISBN: 978-1-61278-353-6
LCCN: 2013950756

Cover design: Tyler Ottinger
Cover photo: Stefano Spaziani

PRINTED IN THE UNITED STATES OF AMERICA

# TABLE OF CONTENTS

CHAPTER ONE
Homily, Palm Sunday   *9*

CHAPTER TWO
General Audience, Wednesday of Holy Week   *15*

CHAPTER THREE
Homily, Holy Thursday   *21*

CHAPTER FOUR
Way of the Cross at the Colosseum Address,
Good Friday   *23*

CHAPTER FIVE
Homily, Holy Saturday   *25*

CHAPTER SIX
*Regina Caeli* Address, Easter Monday   *31*

CHAPTER SEVEN
General Audience, Wednesday within
the Octave of Easter   *33*

CHAPTER EIGHT
*Regina Caeli* Address, Second Sunday of Easter —
Divine Mercy Sunday   *39*

CHAPTER NINE
Homily, Second Sunday of Easter —
Divine Mercy Sunday   *43*

CHAPTER TEN
General Audience, Wednesday of the Second Week
of Easter   *49*

CHAPTER ELEVEN
*Regina Caeli* Address, Third Sunday of Easter   *53*

CHAPTER TWELVE
Homily, Third Sunday of Easter  *57*

CHAPTER THIRTEEN
General Audience, Wednesday of the Third Week
of Easter  *63*

CHAPTER FOURTEEN
*Regina Caeli* Address, Fourth Sunday of Easter  *67*

CHAPTER FIFTEEN
Homily, Tuesday of the Fourth Week of Easter  *71*

CHAPTER SIXTEEN
General Audience, Wednesday of the Fourth Week
of Easter  *75*

CHAPTER SEVENTEEN
Homily, Fifth Sunday of Easter  *81*

CHAPTER EIGHTEEN
Homily, Sixth Sunday of Easter  *85*

CHAPTER NINETEEN
General Audience, Wednesday of the Sixth Week
of Easter  *91*

CHAPTER TWENTY
Homily, Seventh Sunday of Easter  *95*

CHAPTER TWENTY-ONE
General Audience, Wednesday of the Seventh Week
of Easter  *101*

CHAPTER TWENTY-TWO
Homily, Pentecost Sunday  *107*

*Editor's note: The material in this book is derived from catechesis given by Pope Francis during homilies and audiences from March 24, 2013 (Palm Sunday) to May 19, 2013 (Pentecost). The texts have been edited slightly to facilitate presentation in book form. The date each address was originally presented, along with other pertinent information, is annotated in the footnotes.*

# Chapter One

# Homily,[1]
# Palm Sunday

Jesus enters Jerusalem. The crowd of disciples accompanies him in a festive mood, their garments are stretched out before him, there is talk of the miracles he has accomplished, and loud praises are heard: "Blessed is the King who comes in the name of the Lord. Peace in heaven and glory in the highest!" (Lk 19:38).

Crowds, celebrating, praise, blessing, peace: joy fills the air. Jesus has awakened great hopes, especially in the hearts of the simple, the humble, the poor, the forgotten — those who do not matter in the eyes of the world. He understands human sufferings, he has shown the face of God's mercy, and he has bent down to heal body and soul.

This is Jesus. This is his heart, which looks to all of us — to our sicknesses, to our sins. The love of Jesus is great. And thus he enters Jerusalem, with this love, and looks at us. It is a beautiful scene, full of light — the light of the love of Jesus, the love of his heart — of joy, of celebration.

At the beginning of Mass, we too repeated it. We waved our palms, our olive branches. We too welcomed

---

1. Celebration of Palm Sunday of the Passion of Our Lord and Twenty-eighth World Youth Day; March 24, 2013; St. Peter's Square.

Jesus; we too expressed our joy at accompanying him, at knowing him to be close, present in us and among us as a friend, a brother, and also as a King: that is, a shining beacon for our lives. Jesus is God, but he lowered himself to walk with us. He is our friend, our brother. He illumines our path here. And in this way we have welcomed him today. And here is the first word that I wish to say to you: *joy*! Do not be men and women of sadness: a Christian can never be sad! Never give way to discouragement! Ours is not a joy born of having many possessions, but from having encountered a Person: Jesus, in our midst; it is born from knowing that with him we are never alone, even at difficult moments, even when our life's journey comes up against problems and obstacles that seem insurmountable — and there are so many of them! And in this moment the enemy, the devil, comes, often disguised as an angel, and slyly speaks his word to us. Do not listen to him! Let us follow Jesus! We accompany, we follow Jesus, but above all we know that he accompanies us and carries us on his shoulders. This is our joy, this is the hope that we must bring to this world. Please do not let yourselves be robbed of hope! Do not let hope be stolen! The hope that Jesus gives us.

Why does Jesus enter Jerusalem? Or better: how does Jesus enter Jerusalem? The crowds acclaim him as King. And he does not deny it, he does not tell them to be silent (cf. Lk 19:39–40). But what kind of a King is Jesus? Let us take a look at him: he is riding on a donkey, he is not accompanied by a court, he is not surrounded by an army as a symbol of power. He is received by humble people, simple folk who have the sense to see something more in Jesus; they have that sense of the faith that says: here is the Savior. Jesus does not enter the Holy City to receive the honors reserved to earthly kings, to the powerful, to rulers; he enters to be scourged, insulted, and abused, as Isaiah foretold in the First Reading (cf. Is 50:6). He enters to receive a crown of thorns, a staff, a purple robe: his kingship becomes an object of derision. He enters to climb Calvary, carrying his burden of wood. And this brings us to the second word: *Cross*. Jesus enters Jerusalem in order to die on the Cross. And it is precisely here that his kingship shines forth in godly fashion: his royal throne is the wood of the Cross! It reminds me of what Pope Benedict XVI said to the Cardinals: you are princes, but of a king crucified. That is the throne of Jesus. Jesus takes it upon himself.... Why the Cross? Because Jesus takes upon himself the evil, the filth, the sin of the world, including the sin of all of us, and he cleanses it, he cleanses it with his blood, with the mercy and the love of God. Let us look around: how many wounds are inflicted upon humanity by evil! Wars, violence, economic conflicts that hit the weakest, greed for money that you can't take with you and have to leave. When we were small, our grandmother used to say: a shroud has no pocket. Love of power, corruption, divisions, crimes against human life and against creation! And — as each one of us knows and is aware — our personal sins: our failures in love and respect toward God, toward our neighbor, and toward the whole of creation. Jesus on the Cross feels the whole weight of the evil, and with the force of God's love he conquers it, he defeats it with his Resurrection. This is the good that Jesus does for us on the throne of the Cross. Christ's Cross embraced with love never leads to sadness, but to joy, to the joy of having been saved and of doing a little of what he did on the day of his death.

Today, in this Square, there are many young people: for twenty-eight years Palm Sunday has been World Youth Day! Dear young people, I saw you in the procession as you were coming in; I think of you celebrating around Jesus, waving your olive branches. I think of you crying out his name and expressing your joy at being with him! You have an important part in the celebration of faith! You bring us the joy of faith, and you tell us that we must live the faith

> Christ's Cross embraced with love never leads to sadness, but to joy, to the joy of having been saved and of doing a little of what he did on the day of his death.

with a young heart, always: a young heart, even at the age of seventy or eighty. Dear young people! With Christ, the heart never grows old! Yet all of us — all of you — know very well that the King whom we follow and who accompanies us is very special: he is a King who loves even to the Cross and who teaches us to serve and to love. And you are not ashamed of his Cross! On the contrary, you embrace it, because you have understood that it is in giving ourselves, in giving ourselves, in emerging from ourselves, that we have true joy and that, with his love, God conquered evil.

You carry the Pilgrim Cross through all the continents, along the highways of the world! You carry it in response to Jesus' call: "Go, make disciples of all nations" (Mt 28:19), which is the theme of World Youth Day this year. You carry it so as to tell everyone that on the Cross Jesus knocked down the wall of enmity that divides people and nations, and he brought reconciliation and peace. Dear friends, I too am setting out on a journey with you, starting today, in the footsteps of Bl. John Paul II and of Pope Benedict XVI. We are already close to the next stage of this great pilgrimage of the Cross. I look forward joyfully to next July in Rio de Janeiro! I will see you in that great city in Brazil! Prepare well — prepare spiritually above all — in your communities, so that our gathering in Rio may be a sign of faith for the whole world. Young people must say to the world: to follow Christ is good; to go with Christ is good; the message of Christ is good; emerging from ourselves, to the ends of the earth and of existence, to take Jesus there, is good! Three points, then: joy, Cross, young people.

Let us ask the intercession of the Virgin Mary. She teaches us the joy of meeting Christ, the love with which we must look to the foot of the Cross, the enthusiasm of the young heart with which we must follow him during this Holy Week and throughout our lives. May it be so.

# Chapter Two

# GENERAL AUDIENCE,[1]
# WEDNESDAY OF HOLY WEEK

I am glad to welcome all to my first General Audience. With deep gratitude and reverence I take up the "witness" from the hands of Pope Benedict XVI, my beloved Predecessor. After Easter we shall resume the catecheses for the Year of Faith. Today, I would like to reflect a little on Holy Week. We began this Week with Palm Sunday — the heart of the whole Liturgical Year — in which we accompany Jesus in his Passion, death, and Resurrection.

But what does living Holy Week mean to us? What does following Jesus on his journey to Calvary, on his way to the Cross and the Resurrection mean? In his earthly mission, Jesus walked the roads of the Holy Land; he called twelve simple people to stay with him, to share his journey, and to continue his mission. He chose them from among the people full of faith in God's promises. He spoke to all without distinction: the great and the lowly, the rich young man and the poor widow, the powerful and the weak; he brought God's mercy and forgiveness; he healed, he comforted, he understood; he gave hope; he brought to all the presence of God who cares

---

1. March 27, 2013; St. Peter's Square.

for every man and every woman, just as a good father and a good mother care for each one of their children.

God does not wait for us to go to him but it is he who moves toward us, without calculation, without quantification. That is what God is like. He always takes the first step, he comes toward us.

Jesus lived the daily reality of the most ordinary people: he was moved as he faced the crowd that seemed like a flock without a shepherd; he wept before the sorrow that Martha and Mary felt at the death of their brother, Lazarus; he called a publican to be his disciple; he also suffered betrayal by a friend. In him God has given us the certitude that he is with us, he is among us. "Foxes," he, Jesus, said, "have holes, and birds of the air have nests, but the Son of man has nowhere to lay his head" (Mt 8:20). Jesus has no house, because his house is the people, it is we who are his dwelling place, his mission is to open God's doors to all, to be the presence of God's love.

In Holy Week we live the crowning moment of this journey, of this plan of love that runs through the entire history of the relations between God and humanity. Jesus enters Jerusalem to take his last step with which he sums up the whole of his existence. He gives himself without reserve, he keeps nothing for himself, not even life. At the Last Supper, with his friends, he breaks the bread and passes the cup around "for us." The Son of God offers himself to us, he puts his Body and his Blood into our hands, so as to be with us always, to dwell among us. And in the Garden of Olives, and likewise in the trial before Pilate, he puts up no resistance, he gives himself; he is the suffering Servant, foretold by Isaiah, who empties himself, even unto death (cf. Is 53:12).

Jesus does not experience this love that leads to his sacrifice passively or as a fatal destiny. He does not, of course, conceal his deep human distress as he faces a violent death, but with absolute trust commends himself to the Father. Jesus gave himself up to death voluntarily in order to reciprocate the love of God the Father, in perfect union with his will, to demonstrate his love for us. On the Cross Jesus "loved me and gave himself for me" (Gal 2:20). Each one of us can say: "he loved me and gave himself for me." Each one can say this is "for me."

What is the meaning of all this for us? It means that this is my, your, and our road too. Living Holy Week, following Jesus not only with the emotion of the heart; living Holy Week, following Jesus means learning to come out of ourselves — as I said last Sunday — in order to go to meet others, to go toward the outskirts of existence, to be the first to take a step toward our brothers and our sisters, especially those who are the most distant, those who are forgotten, those who are most in need of understanding, comfort, and help. There is such a great need to bring the living presence of Jesus, merciful and full of love!

Living Holy Week means entering ever more deeply into the logic of God, into the logic of the Cross, which is not primarily that of suffering and death, but rather that of love and of the gift of self, which brings life. It means entering into the logic of the Gospel. Following and accompanying Christ, staying with him, demands "coming out of ourselves," requires us to be outgoing; to come out of ourselves, out of a dreary way of living faith that has become a habit, out of the temptation to withdraw into our own plans, which end by shutting out God's creative action.

God came out of himself to come among us, he pitched his tent among us to bring to us his mercy that saves and gives hope. Nor must we be satisfied with staying in the pen of the ninety-nine sheep if we want to follow him and to remain with him; we too must "go out" with him to seek the lost sheep, the one that has strayed the farthest. Be sure to remember: coming out of ourselves, just as Jesus, just as God came out of himself in Jesus and Jesus came out of himself for all of us.

Someone might say to me: "but Father, I don't have time," "I have so many things to do," "it's difficult," "what can I do with my feebleness and my sins, with so many things?" We are often satisfied with a few prayers, with a distracted and sporadic participation in Sunday Mass, with a few charitable acts; but we do not have the courage "to come out" to bring Christ to others. We are a bit like St. Peter. As soon as Jesus speaks of his Passion, death, and Resurrection, of the gift of himself, of love for all, the Apostle takes him aside and reproaches him. What Jesus says upsets his plans, seems unacceptable, threatens the security he had built for himself, his idea of the Messiah. And Jesus looks at his disciples and addresses to Peter what may possibly be the harshest words in the Gospels: "Get behind me, Satan! For you are not on the side of God, but of men" (Mk 8:33). God always thinks with mercy: do not forget this. God always thinks mercifully. He is the merciful Father! God thinks like the father waiting for the son and goes to meet him, he spots him coming when he is still far off....

What does this mean? That he went every day to see if his son was coming home: this

> God always thinks with mercy: do not forget this. God always thinks mercifully. He is the merciful Father!

is our merciful Father. It indicates that he was waiting for him with longing on the terrace of his house. God thinks like the Samaritan who did not pass by the unfortunate man, pitying him or looking at him from the other side of the road, but helped him without asking for anything in return; without asking whether he was a Jew, a pagan, or a Samaritan, whether he was rich or poor: he asked for nothing. He went to help him: God is like this. God thinks like the shepherd who lays down his life in order to defend and save his sheep.

Holy Week is a time of grace that the Lord gives us *to open the doors* of our heart, of our life, of our parishes — what a pity so many parishes are closed! — of the movements, of the associations; and "to come out" in order to meet others, to make ourselves close, to bring them the light and joy of our faith. To come out always! And to do so with God's love and tenderness, with respect and with patience, knowing that God takes our hands, our feet, our heart, and guides them and makes all our actions fruitful.

I hope that we all will live these days well, following the Lord courageously, carrying within us a ray of his love for all those we meet.

# Chapter Three

# HOMILY,[1]
# HOLY THURSDAY

This is moving. Jesus, washing the feet of his disciples. Peter didn't understand it at all, he refused. But Jesus explained it for him. Jesus — God — did this! He himself explains to his disciples: "Do you know what I have done to you? You call me Teacher and Lord — and you are right, for that is what I am. So if I, your Lord and Teacher, have washed your feet, you also ought to wash one another's feet. For I have set you an example, that you also should do as I have done to you" (Jn 13:12–15).

It is the Lord's example: he is the most important, and he washes feet, because with us what is highest must be at the service of others. This is a symbol. It is a sign, right? Washing feet means: "I am at your service." And with us, too, don't we have to wash each other's feet day after day? But what does this mean? That all of us must help one another. Sometimes I am angry with someone or other … but … let it go, let it go, and if he or she asks you a favor, do it.

---

1. Mass of the Lord's Supper; March 28, 2013; Prison for Minors "Casal del Marmo," Rome.

Help one another: this is what Jesus teaches us, and this is what I am doing, and doing with all my heart, because it is my duty. As a priest and a bishop, I must be at your service. But it is a duty that comes from my heart: I love it. I love this, and I love to do it because that is what the Lord has taught me to do. But you, too, help one another: help one another always. One another. In this way, by helping one another, we will do some good.

> As a priest and a bishop, I must be at your service. But it is a duty that comes from my heart: I love it.

Now we will perform this ceremony of washing feet, and let us think, let each one of us think: "Am I really willing, willing to serve, to help others?" Let us think about this, just this. And let us think that this sign is a caress of Jesus, which Jesus gives, because this is the real reason why Jesus came: to serve, to help us.

Chapter Four

# Way of the Cross at the Colosseum Address,[1] Good Friday

Thank you for having taken part in these moments of deep prayer. I also thank those who have accompanied us through the media, especially the sick and elderly.

I do not wish to add too many words. One word should suffice this evening, that is the Cross itself. The Cross is the word through which God has responded to evil in the world. Sometimes it may seem as though God does not react to evil, as if he is silent. And yet, God has spoken, he has replied, and his answer is the Cross of Christ: a word that is love, mercy, forgiveness. It also reveals a judgment, namely that God, in judging us, loves us. Let us remember this: God judges us by loving us. If I embrace his love then I am saved, if I refuse it, then I am condemned, not by him, but by my own self, because God never condemns, he only loves and saves.

Dear brothers and sisters, the word of the Cross is also the answer that Christians offer in the face of evil, the evil that continues to work in us and around us. Christians must respond to evil with good, taking the

---

1. March 29, 2013; Palatine Hill.

Cross upon themselves as Jesus did. This evening we have
heard the witness given by our Lebanese brothers and
sisters: they composed these beautiful
prayers and meditations. We extend
our heartfelt gratitude to them for this
work and for the witness they offer.
We were able to see this when Pope
Benedict visited Lebanon: we saw
the beauty and the strong bond of communion joining
Christians together in that land and the friendship of our
Muslim brothers and sisters and so many others. That
occasion was a sign to the Middle East and to the whole
world: a sign of hope.

> Let us remember this: God judges us by loving us.

We now continue this *Via Crucis* in our daily lives.
Let us walk together along the Way of the Cross and let
us do so carrying in our hearts this word of love and forgiveness. Let us go forward waiting for the Resurrection
of Jesus, who loves us so much. He is all love!

# Chapter Five

# Homily,[1]
# Holy Saturday

In the Gospel of this radiant night of the Easter Vigil, we first meet the women who go to the tomb of Jesus with spices to anoint his body (cf. Lk 24:1–3). They go to perform an act of compassion, a traditional act of affection and love for a dear departed person, just as we would. They had followed Jesus, they had listened to his words, they had felt understood by him in their dignity, and they had accompanied him to the very end, to Calvary and to the moment when he was taken down from the Cross.

We can imagine their feelings as they make their way to the tomb: a certain sadness, sorrow that Jesus had left them, he had died, his life had come to an end. Life would now go on as before. Yet the women continued to feel love, the love for Jesus, which now led them to his tomb. But at this point, something completely new and unexpected happens, something that upsets their hearts and their plans, something that will upset their whole life: they see the stone removed from before the tomb, they draw near, and they do not find the Lord's body.

---

1. Easter Vigil; March 30, 2013; Vatican Basilica.

It is an event that leaves them perplexed, hesitant, full of questions: "What happened?" "What is the meaning of all this?" (cf. Lk 24:4). Doesn't the same thing also happen to us when something completely new occurs in our everyday life? We stop short, we don't understand, we don't know what to do. *Newness* often makes us fearful, including the newness that God brings us, the newness that God asks of us. We are like the Apostles in the Gospel: often we would prefer to hold on to our own security, to stand in front of a tomb, to think about someone who has died, someone who ultimately lives on only as a memory, like the great historical figures from the past. We are afraid of God's surprises. Dear brothers and sisters, we are afraid of God's surprises! He always surprises us! The Lord is like that.

Dear brothers and sisters, let us not be closed to the newness that God wants to bring into our lives! Are we often weary, disheartened, and sad? Do we feel weighed down by our sins? Do we think that we won't be able to cope? Let us not close our hearts, let us not lose confidence, let us never give up: there are no situations that God cannot change, there is no sin that he cannot forgive if only we open ourselves to him.

Let us return to the Gospel, to the women, and take one step further. They find the tomb empty, the body of Jesus is not there, something new has happened, but all this still doesn't tell them anything certain: it raises questions; it leaves them confused, without offering an answer. And suddenly there are two men in dazzling clothes who say: "Why do you look for the living among the dead? He is not here; but has risen" (Lk 24:5–6). What was a simple act, done surely out of love — going to the tomb — has now turned into an event, a truly life-changing event. Nothing remains as it was before, not only in the lives of those women, but also in our own lives and in the history of mankind. Jesus is not dead, he has risen, he is *alive*! He does not simply return to life; rather, he is life itself, because he is the Son of God, the living God (cf. Num 14:21–28; Deut 5:26; Josh 3:10).

Jesus no longer belongs to the past, but lives in the present and is projected toward the future; Jesus is the everlasting "today" of God. This is how the newness of God appears to the women, the disciples, and all of us: as victory over sin, evil, and death, over everything that crushes life and makes it seem less human. And this is a message meant for me and for you, dear sister, for you, dear brother. How often does Love have to tell us: Why do you look for the living among the dead? Our daily problems and worries can wrap us up in ourselves, in sadness and bitterness … and that is where death is. That is not the place to look for the One who is alive!

Let the Risen Jesus enter your life, welcome him as a friend, with trust: he is life! If up till now you have kept him at a distance, step forward. He will receive you with open arms. If you have been indifferent, take a risk: you won't be disappointed. If following him seems difficult, don't be afraid, trust him, be confident that he is close to you, he is with you, and he will give you the peace you are looking for and the strength to live as he would have you do.

There is one last little element that I would like to emphasize in the Gospel for this Easter Vigil. The women encounter the newness of God. Jesus has risen; he is alive! But faced with the empty tomb and the two men in brilliant clothes, their first reaction is one of fear: "they were terrified and bowed their faces to the ground," St. Luke tells us — they didn't even have courage to look. But when they hear the message of the Resurrection, they accept it in faith. And the two men in dazzling clothes tell them something of crucial importance: remember. "'Remember how he told you, while he was still in Galilee,'... And they remembered his words" (Lk 24:6, 8).

> To remember what God has done and continues to do for me, for us, to remember the road we have traveled; this is what opens our hearts to hope for the future.

This is the invitation to *remember* their encounter with Jesus, to remember his words, his actions, his life; and it is precisely this loving remembrance of their experience with the Master that enables the women to master their fear and to bring the message of the Resurrection to the Apostles and all the others (cf. Lk 24:9). To remember what God has done and continues to do for me, for us, to remember the road we have traveled; this is what opens our hearts to hope for the future. May we learn to remember everything that God has done in our lives.

On this radiant night, let us invoke the intercession of the Virgin Mary, who treasured all these events in her heart (cf. Lk 2:19,51), and ask the Lord to give us a share in his Resurrection. May he open us to the newness that transforms, to the beautiful surprises of God. May he make us men and women capable of remembering all that he has done in our own lives and in the history of our world. May he help us to feel his presence as the one who is alive and at work in our midst. And may he teach us each day, dear brothers and sisters, not to look among the dead for the Living One. Amen.

# Chapter Six

## *REGINA CAELI* ADDRESS,[1]
## EASTER MONDAY

G ood Morning and a Happy Easter to all! I thank
you for coming here today, too, in such large
numbers, to share in the joy of Easter, the cen-
tral mystery of our faith. May the power of Christ's Resurrection reach every person — especially those who are
suffering — and all the situations most in need of trust
and hope.

Christ has fully triumphed over evil once and for
all, but it is up to us, to the people of every epoch, to
welcome this victory into our life and into the actual
situations of history and society. For this reason, it seems
to me important to emphasize what we ask God today
in the liturgy. "O God, who gives constant increase / to
your Church by new offspring, / grant that your servants
may hold fast in their lives / to the Sacrament they have
received in faith" (Collect, Monday within the Octave of
Easter).

It is true, yes, Baptism that makes us children of
God and the Eucharist that unites us to Christ must become life; that is, they must be expressed in attitudes,
behavior, gestures, and decisions. The grace contained

---

1. April 1, 2013; St. Peter's Square.

in the Sacraments of Easter is an enormous potential for the renewal of our personal existence, of family life, of social relations. However, everything passes through the human heart: if I let myself be touched by the grace of the Risen Christ, if I let him change me in that aspect of mine that is not good, which can hurt me and others, I allow the victory of Christ to be affirmed in my life, to broaden its beneficial action. This is the power of grace! Without grace we can do nothing. Without grace we can do nothing! And with the grace of Baptism and of Eucharistic Communion I can become an instrument of God's mercy, of that beautiful mercy of God.

Without grace we can do nothing!

To express in life the sacrament we have received: dear brothers and sisters, this is our daily duty, but I would also say our daily joy! The joy of feeling we are instruments of Christ's grace, like branches of the vine that is Christ himself, brought to life by the sap of his Spirit!

Let us pray together, in the name of the dead and Risen Lord and through the intercession of Mary Most Holy, that the Paschal Mystery may work profoundly within us and in our time so that hatred may give way to love, falsehood to truth, revenge to forgiveness, and sadness to joy.

## Chapter Seven

## GENERAL AUDIENCE,[1]
## WEDNESDAY WITHIN
## THE OCTAVE OF EASTER

Now let us take up the catecheses of the Year of Faith. In the *Creed*, we repeat these words: "and rose again on the third day in accordance with the Scriptures." This is the very event that we are celebrating: the Resurrection of Jesus, the center of the Christian message that has echoed from the beginning and was passed on so that it would come down to us. St. Paul wrote to the Christians of Corinth: "I delivered to you as of first importance what I also received, that Christ died for our sins in accordance with the scriptures, that he was buried, that he was raised on the third day in accordance with the scriptures, and that he appeared to Cephas, then to the Twelve" (1 Cor 15:3–5). This brief profession of faith proclaims the Paschal Mystery itself with the first appearances of the Risen One to Peter and the Twelve: *the death and Resurrection of Jesus are the very heart of our hope.*

Without this faith in the death and Resurrection of Jesus, our hope would be weak; but it would not even be hope; or, precisely, the death and Resurrection of Jesus

---

1. April 3, 2013; St. Peter's Square.

are the heart of our hope. The Apostle said: "If Christ has not been raised, your faith is futile and you are still in your sins" (v. 17). Unfortunately, efforts have often been made to blur faith in the Resurrection of Jesus, and doubts have crept in, even among believers. It is a little like that "rosewater" faith, as we say; it is not a strong faith. And this is due to superficiality, and sometimes to indifference, busy as we are with a thousand things considered more important than faith, or because we have a view of life that is solely horizontal. However, it is the Resurrection itself that opens us to greater hope, for it opens our life and the life of the world to the eternal future of God, to full happiness, to the certainty that evil, sin, and death may be overcome. And this leads to living daily situations with greater trust, to facing them with courage and determination. Christ's Resurrection illuminates these everyday situations with a new light. The Resurrection of Christ is our strength!

But how was the truth of faith in Christ's Resurrection passed down to us? There are two kinds of testimony in the New Testament: some are in the form of a profession of faith, that is, of concise formulas that indicate the center of faith; while others are in the form of an account of the event of the Resurrection and of the facts connected with it.

The former, in the form of a profession of faith, for example, is the one we have just heard, or that of the Letter to the Romans, in which St. Paul wrote: "if you confess with your lips that 'Jesus is Lord!' and believe in your heart that God raised him from the dead, you will be saved" (10:9). From the Church's very first steps, faith in the Mystery of the death and Resurrection of Christ is firm and clear. Today, however, I would like to reflect on the latter, on the testimonies in the form of a narrative that we find in the Gospels. First of all, let us note that the first witnesses of this event were the women. At dawn, they went to the tomb to anoint Jesus' body and found the first sign: the empty tomb (cf. Mk 16:1). Their meeting with a messenger of God followed. He announced: "Jesus of Nazareth, the Crucified One, has risen, he is not here" (cf. vv. 5–6). The women were motivated by love and were able to accept this announcement with faith: they believed and passed it on straight away, they did not keep it to themselves but passed it on.

They could not contain their joy in knowing that Jesus was alive, or the hope that filled their hearts. This should happen in our lives too. Let us feel the joy of being Christian! We believe in the Risen One who conquered evil and death! Let us have the courage to "come out of ourselves" to take this joy and this light to all the places of our life! The Resurrection of Christ is our greatest certainty; he is our most precious treasure! How can we not share this treasure, this certainty with others? It is not only for us, it is to be passed on, to be shared with others. Our testimony is precisely this.

Another point: in the profession of faith in the New Testament, only men are recorded as witnesses of the Resurrection — the Apostles, but not the women. This is because, according to the Judaic Law of that time, women and children could not bear a trustworthy, credible witness. Instead, in the Gospels, women play a fundamental lead role. Here we can grasp an element in favor of the historicity of the Resurrection: if it was an invented event, in the context of that time it would not have been linked with the evidence of women. Instead, the Evangelists simply recounted what happened: women were the first witnesses. This implies that God does not choose in accordance with human criteria: the first witnesses of the birth of Jesus were shepherds, simple, humble people; the first witnesses of the Resurrection were women. And this is beautiful. This is part of the mission of women; of mothers, of women! Witnessing to their children, to their grandchildren, that Jesus is alive, is living, is risen. Mothers and women, carry on witnessing to this! It is the heart that counts for God, how open to him we are, whether we are like trusting children.

However, this also makes us think about how women, in the Church and on the journey of faith, had and still have today a special role in opening the doors to the Lord, in following him, and in communicating his Face, for the gaze of faith is always in need of the simple and profound gaze of love.

The Apostles and disciples find it harder to believe. The women, not so. Peter runs to the tomb but stops at the empty tomb; Thomas has to touch the wounds on Jesus' body with his hands. On our way of faith it is also important to know and to feel that God loves us and to not be afraid to love him. Faith is professed with the lips and with the heart, with words and with love.

After his appearances to the women, others follow. Jesus makes himself present in a new way, he is the Crucified One but his body is glorified; he did not return to earthly life, but returned in a new condition. At first, they do not recognize him, and it is only through his words and gestures that their eyes are opened. The meeting with the Risen One transforms, it gives faith fresh strength and a steadfast foundation. For us, too, there are many signs through which the Risen One makes himself known: Sacred Scripture, the Eucharist, the other Sacraments, charity, all those acts of love that bring a ray of the Risen One. Let us permit ourselves to be illuminated by Christ's Resurrection, let him transform us with his power, so that through us too the signs of death may give way to signs of life in the world.

I see that there are large numbers of young people in the square. There you are! I say to you, carry this certainty ahead: the Lord is alive and walks beside you through life. This is your mission! Carry this hope onward. May you be anchored to this hope: this anchor that is in heaven; hold the rope firmly, be anchored, and carry hope forward. You, witnesses of Jesus, pass on the witness that Jesus is alive, and this will give us hope, it will give hope to this world, which has aged somewhat, because of wars, because of evil, and because of sin. Press on, young people!

> Carry this hope onward. May you be anchored to this hope: this anchor that is in heaven; hold the rope firmly, be anchored, and carry hope forward.

# Chapter Eight

# *REGINA CAELI* ADDRESS,[1]
## SECOND SUNDAY OF EASTER —
## DIVINE MERCY SUNDAY

O n this Sunday that brings the Octave of Easter
to a close, I renew to everyone my good wishes
for Easter in the very words of the Risen Jesus:
"*Peace be with you*" (Jn 20:19, 21, 26). This is not a greeting, nor even a simple good wish: it is a gift, indeed, *the*
precious gift that Christ offered his disciples after he had
passed through death and hell.

He gives peace, as he had promised: "Peace I leave
with you; my peace I give to you; not as the world gives
do I give to you" (Jn 14:27). This peace is the fruit of the
victory of God's love over evil, it is the fruit of forgiveness. And it really is like this: true peace, that profound
peace, comes from experiencing God's mercy. Today is
Divine Mercy Sunday, as Bl. John Paul II — who closed
his eyes to the world on the eve of this very day — wanted it to be.

John's Gospel tells us that Jesus appeared twice to
the Apostles enclosed in the Upper Room: the first time
on the evening of the Resurrection itself, and on that
occasion Thomas, who said unless I see and touch I will

---

1. April 7, 2013; St. Peter's Square.

not believe, was absent. The second time, eight days later, Thomas was there as well. And Jesus said, speaking directly to him, I invite you to look at my wounds, to touch them; then Thomas exclaimed: "My Lord and my God!" (Jn 20:28). So Jesus said: "Have you believed because you have seen me? Blessed are those who have not seen and yet believe" (v. 29); and who were those who believed without seeing?

Other disciples, other men and women of Jerusalem, who, on the testimony of the Apostles and the women, believed, even though they had not met the Risen Jesus. This is a very important word about faith; we can call it *the beatitude of faith*. Blessed are those who have not seen but have believed: this is the beatitude of faith! In every epoch and in every place, blessed are those who, on the strength of the word of God, proclaimed in the Church and witnessed by Christians, believe that Jesus Christ is the love of God incarnate, Mercy incarnate. And this applies for each one of us!

As well as his peace, Jesus gave the Apostles the Holy Spirit so that they could spread the forgiveness of sins in the world, that forgiveness that only God can give and that came at the price of the Blood of the Son (cf. Jn 20:21–23). The Church is sent by the Risen Christ to pass on to men and women the forgiveness of sins and thereby make the Kingdom of love grow, to sow peace in hearts so that they may also be strengthened in relationships, in every society, in institutions.

And the Spirit of the Risen Christ drove out fear from the Apostles' hearts and impelled them to leave the

Upper Room in order to spread the Gospel. Let us, too, have greater courage in witnessing to our faith in the Risen Christ! We must not be afraid of being Christian and living as Christians! We must have this courage to go and proclaim the Risen Christ, for he is our peace, he made peace with his love, with his forgiveness, with his Blood, and with his mercy.

> We must not be afraid of being Christian and living as Christians!

Dear friends, this afternoon I shall celebrate the Eucharist in the Basilica of St. John Lateran, which is the Cathedral of the Bishop of Rome. Together, let us pray the Virgin Mary that she help us, Bishop and People, to walk in faith and charity, ever trusting in the Lord's mercy: he always awaits us, loves us, has pardoned us with his Blood, and pardons us every time we go to him to ask his forgiveness. Let us trust in his mercy!

# Chapter Nine

# HOMILY,[1]
## SECOND SUNDAY OF EASTER —
## DIVINE MERCY SUNDAY

I t is with joy that I am celebrating the Eucharist for the first time in this Lateran Basilica, the Cathedral of the Bishop of Rome. I greet all of you with great affection: my very dear Cardinal Vicar, the auxiliary bishops, the diocesan presbyterate, the deacons, the men and women religious, and all the lay faithful. I also greet the Mayor, his wife and all the authorities present. Together, let us walk in the light of the risen Lord.

1. Today we are celebrating the Second Sunday of Easter, also known as "Divine Mercy Sunday." What a beautiful truth of faith this is for our lives: the mercy of God! God's love for us is so great, so deep; it is an unfailing love, one that always takes us by the hand and supports us, lifts us up, and leads us on.

2. In today's Gospel, the Apostle Thomas personally experiences this mercy of God, which has a concrete face, the face of Jesus, the Risen Jesus. Thomas does not believe it when the other Apostles tell him: "We have seen the Lord." It isn't enough for him that Jesus had foretold

---

1. Papal Mass for the Possession of the Chair of the Bishop of Rome; April 7, 2013; Basilica of St. John Lateran.

it, promised it: "On the third day I will rise." He wants to
see, he wants to put his hand in the place of the nails and
in Jesus' side. And how does Jesus react? With patience:
Jesus does not abandon Thomas in his stubborn unbelief;
he gives him a week's time, he does not close the door,
he waits. And Thomas acknowledges his own poverty,
his little faith. "My Lord and my God!" With this simple
yet faith-filled invocation, he responds to Jesus' patience.
He lets himself be enveloped by divine mercy; he sees it
before his eyes, in the wounds of Christ's hands and feet
and in his open side, and he discovers trust: he is a new
man, no longer an unbeliever, but a believer.

Let us also remember Peter: three times he denied
Jesus, precisely when he should have been closest to him;
and when he hits bottom he meets the gaze of Jesus who
patiently, wordlessly, says to him: "Peter, don't be afraid
of your weakness, trust in me." Peter understands, he
feels the loving gaze of Jesus, and he weeps. How beautiful is this gaze of Jesus — how much tenderness is there!
Brothers and sisters, let us never lose trust in the patience
and mercy of God!

Let us think, too, of the two disciples on the way to
Emmaus: their sad faces, their barren journey, their de-
spair. But Jesus does not abandon them: he walks beside
them, and not only that! Patiently, he explains the Scriptures that spoke of him, and he stays to share a meal with
them. This is God's way of doing things: he is not impa-
tient like us, who often want everything all at once, even
in our dealings with other people. God is patient with us
because he loves us, and those who love are able to un-

derstand, to hope, to inspire confidence; they do not give up, they do not burn bridges, they are able to forgive. Let us remember this in our lives as Christians: God always waits for us, even when we have left him behind! He is never far from us, and if we return to him, he is ready to embrace us.

> God always waits for us, even when we have left him behind!

I am always struck when I reread the parable of the merciful Father; it impresses me because it always gives me great hope. Think of that younger son who was in the Father's house, who was loved; and yet he wants his part of the inheritance; he goes off, spends everything, hits rock bottom, where he could not be more distant from the Father, yet when he is at his lowest, he misses the warmth of the Father's house and he goes back. And the Father? Had he forgotten the son? No, never. He is there, he sees the son from afar, he was waiting for him every hour of every day, the son was always in his father's heart, even though he had left him, even though he had squandered his whole inheritance, his freedom. The Father, with patience, love, hope, and mercy, had never for a second stopped thinking about him, and as soon as he sees him still far off, he runs out to meet him and embraces him with tenderness, the tenderness of God, without a word of reproach: he has returned! And that is the joy of the Father. In that embrace for his son is all this joy: he has returned! God is always waiting for us; he never grows tired. Jesus shows us this merciful patience of God so that we can regain confidence, hope — always! A great

German theologian, Romano Guardini, said that God responds to our weakness by his patience, and this is the reason for our confidence, our hope (cf. *Glaubenserkenntnis*, Würzburg, 1949, p. 28). It is like a dialogue between our weakness and the patience of God, it is a dialogue that, if we do it, will grant us hope.

3. I would like to emphasize one other thing: God's patience has to call forth in us the courage to return to him, however many mistakes and sins there may be in our life. Jesus tells Thomas to put his hand in the wounds of his hands and his feet, and in his side. We too can enter into the wounds of Jesus; we can actually touch him. This happens every time we receive the sacraments with faith. St. Bernard, in a fine homily, says: "Through the wounds of Jesus I can suck honey from the rock and oil from the flinty rock (cf. Deut 32:13), I can taste and see the goodness of the Lord" (*On the Song of Songs*, 61:4). It is there, in the wounds of Jesus, that we are truly secure; there we encounter the boundless love of his heart. Thomas understood this. St. Bernard goes on to ask: But what can I count on? My own merits? No, "My merit is God's mercy. I am by no means lacking merits as long as he is rich in mercy. If the mercies of the Lord are manifold, I too will abound in merits" (ibid., 5). This is important: the courage to trust in Jesus' mercy, to trust in his patience, to seek refuge always in the wounds of his love. St. Bernard even states: "So what if my conscience gnaws at me for my many sins? 'Where sin has abounded, there grace has abounded all the more' (Rom 5:20)" (ibid.). Maybe someone among us here is thinking: my

sin is so great, I am as far from God as the younger son in the parable, my unbelief is like that of Thomas; I don't have the courage to go back, to believe that God can welcome me and that he is waiting for me, of all people. But God is indeed waiting for you; he asks of you only the courage to go to him. How many times in my pastoral ministry have I heard it said: "Father, I have many sins"; and I have always pleaded: "Don't be afraid, go to him, he is waiting for you, he will take care of everything." We hear many offers from the world around us; but let us take up God's offer instead: his is a caress of love. For God, we are not numbers, we are important, indeed we are the most important thing to him; even if we are sinners, we are what is closest to his heart.

Adam, after his sin, experiences shame, he feels naked, he senses the weight of what he has done; and yet God does not abandon him: if that moment of sin marks the beginning of his exile from God, there is already a promise of return, a possibility of return. God immediately asks: "Adam, where are you?" He seeks him out. Jesus took on our nakedness, he took upon himself the shame of Adam, the nakedness of his sin, in order to wash away our sin: by his wounds we have been healed. Remember what St. Paul says: "What shall I boast of, if not my weakness, my poverty?" Precisely in feeling my sinfulness, in looking at my sins, I can see and encounter God's mercy, his love, and go to him to receive forgiveness.

In my own life, I have so often seen God's merciful countenance, his patience; I have also seen so many people find the courage to enter the wounds of Jesus by saying to him: Lord, I am here, accept my poverty, hide my sin in your wounds, wash it away with your blood. And I have always seen that God did just this — he accepted them, consoled them, cleansed them, loved them.

Dear brothers and sisters, let us be enveloped by the mercy of God; let us trust in his patience, which always gives us more time. Let us find the courage to return to his house, to dwell in his loving wounds, allowing ourselves be loved by him and to encounter his mercy in the sacraments. We will feel his wonderful tenderness, we will feel his embrace, and we too will become more capable of mercy, patience, forgiveness, and love.

Chapter Ten

# General Audience,[1]
# Wednesday of the Second Week
# of Easter

Previously, we reflected on the event of the Resurrection of Jesus, in which the women played a special role. Today, I would like to reflect on its saving capacity. What does the Resurrection mean for our life? And why is our faith in vain without it?

Our faith is founded on Christ's death and Resurrection, just as a house stands on its foundations: if they give way, the whole house collapses. Jesus gave himself on the Cross, taking the burden of our sins upon himself and descending into the abyss of death, then in the Resurrection he triumphed over them, took them away, and opened before us the path to rebirth and to a new life.

St. Peter summed this up at the beginning of his First Letter, as we heard: "Blessed be the God and Father of our Lord Jesus Christ! By his great mercy we have been born anew to a living hope through the Resurrection of Jesus Christ from the dead, and to an inheritance which is imperishable, undefiled, and unfading" (1:3–4).

The Apostle tells us that with the Resurrection of Jesus something absolutely new happens: we are set free

1. April 10, 2013; St. Peter's Square.

from the slavery of sin and become children of God; that is, we are born to new life. When is this accomplished for us? In the sacrament of Baptism. In ancient times, it was customarily received through immersion. The person who was to be baptized walked down into the great basin of the Baptistery, stepping out of his clothes, and the bishop or priest poured water on his head three times, baptizing him in the name of the Father, of the Son, and of the Holy Spirit. Then the baptized person emerged from the basin and put on a new robe, the white one; in other words, by immersing himself in the death and Resurrection of Christ he was born to new life. He had become a son of God. In his Letter to the Romans, St. Paul wrote: "you have received the spirit of sonship. When we cry 'Abba! Father!' it is the Spirit himself bearing witness with our spirit that we are children of God" (Rom 8:15–16).

It is the Spirit himself, whom we received in Baptism, who teaches us, who spurs us to say to God: "Father," or rather, "Abba!" — which means "papa" or ["dad"]. Our God is like this: he is a dad to us. The Holy Spirit creates within us this new condition as children of God. And this is the greatest gift we have received from the Paschal Mystery of Jesus. Moreover, God treats us as children, he understands us, he forgives us, he embraces us, he loves us even when we err. In the Old Testament, the Prophet Isaiah was already affirming that even if a mother could forget her child, God never forgets us at any moment (cf. 49:15). And this is beautiful!

Yet this filial relationship with God is not like a treasure that we keep in a corner of our life, but must be increased. It must be nourished every day with listening to the word of God, with prayer, with participation in the sacraments, especially Reconciliation and the Eucharist, and with love. We can live as children! And this is our dignity — we have the dignity of children. We should behave as true children! This means that every day we must let Christ transform us and conform us to him; it means striving to live as Christians, endeavoring to follow him in spite of seeing our limitations and weaknesses. The temptation to set God aside in order to put ourselves at the center is always at the door, and the experience of sin injures our Christian life, our being children of God. For this reason, we must have the courage of faith not to allow ourselves to be guided by the mentality that tells us: "God is not necessary, he is not important for you," and so forth. It is exactly the opposite: only by behaving as

> The Risen Lord is the hope that never fails, that never disappoints (cf. Rom 5:5). Hope does not let us down — the hope of the Lord!

children of God, without despairing at our shortcomings, at our sins, only by feeling loved by him will our life be new, enlivened by serenity and joy. God is our strength! God is our hope!

Dear brothers and sisters, we must be the first to have this steadfast hope, and we must be a visible, clear, and radiant sign of it for everyone. The Risen Lord is the hope that never fails, that never disappoints (cf. Rom 5:5). Hope does not let us down — the hope of the Lord! How often in our life do hopes vanish, how often do the expectations we have in our heart come to nothing! Our hope as Christians is strong, safe, and sound on this earth, where God has called us to walk, and it is open to eternity because it is founded on God who is always faithful. We must not forget: God is always faithful to us. Being raised with Christ through Baptism, with the gift of faith, an inheritance that is incorruptible, prompts us to seek God's things more often, to think of him more often, and to pray to him more.

Being Christian is not just obeying orders, but means being in Christ, thinking like him, acting like him, loving like him; it means letting him take possession of our life and change it, transform it, and free it from the darkness of evil and sin.

Dear brothers and sisters, let us point out the Risen Christ to those who ask us to account for the hope that is in us (cf. 1 Pet 3:15). Let us point him out with the proclamation of the word, but above all with our lives as people who have been raised. Let us show the joy of being children of God, the freedom that living in Christ gives us, which is true freedom, the freedom that saves us from the slavery of evil, of sin, and of death! Looking at the heavenly homeland, we shall receive new light and fresh strength, both in our commitment and in our daily efforts.

This is a precious service that we must give to this world of ours, which all too often no longer succeeds in raising its gaze on high, no longer succeeds in raising its gaze to God.

# Chapter Eleven

# *REGINA CAELI* ADDRESS,[1]
# THIRD SUNDAY OF EASTER

I would like to reflect briefly on the passage from the Acts of the Apostles that is read in the Liturgy of this Third Sunday of Easter. This text says that the Apostles' first preaching in Jerusalem filled the city with the news that Jesus was truly risen in accordance with the Scriptures and was the Messiah foretold by the Prophets. The chief priests and elders of the city were endeavoring to crush the nascent community of believers in Christ and had the Apostles thrown into jail, ordering them to stop teaching in his name. But Peter and the other eleven answered: "We must obey God rather than men. The God of our fathers raised Jesus … exalted him at his right hand as Leader and Savior…. And we are witnesses to these things, and so is the Holy Spirit whom God has given to those who obey him" (Acts 5:29–32). They therefore had the Apostles scourged and once again ordered them to stop speaking in the name of Jesus. And they went away, as Scripture says, "rejoicing that they were counted worthy to suffer dishonor for the name" of Jesus (v. 41).

---

1. April 14, 2013; St. Peter's Square.

I ask myself: where did the first disciples find the strength to bear this witness? And that is not all: what was the source of their joy and of their courage to preach despite the obstacles and violence? Let us not forget that the Apostles were simple people; they were neither scribes nor doctors of the law, nor did they belong to the class of priests. With their limitations and with the authorities against them, how did they manage to fill Jerusalem with their teaching (cf. Acts 5:28)?

It is clear that only the presence with them of the Risen Lord and the action of the Holy Spirit can explain this fact. The Lord who was with them and the Spirit who was impelling them to preach explain this extraordinary fact. Their faith was based on such a strong personal experience of the dead and Risen Christ that they feared nothing and no one, and they even saw persecution as a cause of honor that enabled them to follow in Jesus' footsteps and to be like him, witnessing with their life.

This history of the first Christian community tells us something very important that applies to the Church in all times and also to us. When a person truly knows Jesus Christ and believes in him, that person experiences his presence in life, as well as the power of his Resurrection, and cannot but communicate this experience. And if this person meets with misunderstanding or adversity, he behaves like Jesus in his Passion: he answers with love and with the power of the truth.

In praying the *Regina Caeli* together, let us ask for the help of Mary Most Holy so that the Church throughout the world may proclaim the Resurrection of the Lord with candor and courage and give credible witness to it with signs of brotherly love. Brotherly love is the clos-est testimony we can give that Jesus is alive with us, that Jesus is risen.

Let us pray in a special way for Christians who are suffering persecution; in our day there are so many Christians who are

Brotherly love is the closest testimony we can give that Jesus is alive with us, that Jesus is risen.

suffering persecution — so, so many, in a great many countries: let us pray for them, with love, from our heart. May they feel the living and comforting presence of the Risen Lord.

# Chapter Twelve

# HOMILY,[1]
## THIRD SUNDAY OF EASTER

It is a joy for me to celebrate Mass in this Basilica. I greet the Archpriest Cardinal James Harvey, and I thank him for the words that he has addressed to me. Along with him, I greet and thank the various institutions that form part of this Basilica, and all of you. We are at the tomb of St. Paul, a great yet humble Apostle of the Lord, who proclaimed him by word, bore witness to him by martyrdom, and worshipped him with all his heart. These are the three key ideas on which I would like to reflect in the light of the word of God that we have heard: proclamation, witness, worship.

In the First Reading, what strikes us is the strength of Peter and the other Apostles. In response to the order to be silent, no longer to teach in the name of Jesus, no longer to proclaim his message, they respond clearly: "We must obey God, rather than men." And they remain undeterred even when flogged, ill-treated, and imprisoned. Peter and the Apostles proclaim courageously, fearlessly, what they have received: the Gospel of Jesus. And we? Are we capable of bringing the word of God into the environment in which we live? Do we know how to speak

---

1. April 14, 2013; Basilica of St. Paul Outside-the-Walls.

of Christ, of what he represents for us, in our families, among the people who form part of our daily lives? Faith is born from listening, and is strengthened by proclamation.

But let us take a further step: the proclamation made by Peter and the Apostles does not merely consist of words: fidelity to Christ affects their whole lives, which are changed, given a new direction, and it is through their lives that they bear witness to the faith and to the proclamation of Christ. In today's Gospel, Jesus asks Peter three times to feed his flock, to feed it with his love, and he prophesies to him: "When you are old, you will stretch out your hands, and another will gird you and carry you where you do not wish to go" (Jn 21:18). These words are addressed first and foremost to those of us who are pastors: we cannot feed God's flock unless we let ourselves be carried by God's will even where we would rather not go, unless we are prepared to bear witness to Christ with the gift of ourselves, unreservedly, not in a calculating way, sometimes even at the cost of our lives. But this also applies to everyone: we all have to proclaim and bear witness to the Gospel.

We should all ask ourselves: How do I bear witness to Christ through my faith? Do I have the courage of Peter and the other Apostles to think, to choose, and to live as a Christian, obedient to God? To be sure, the testimony of faith comes in very many forms, just as in a great fresco, there is a variety of colors and shades; yet they are all important, even those that do not stand out. In God's great plan, every detail is important, even yours, even my humble little witness, even the hidden witness of those who live their faith with simplicity in everyday family relationships, work relationships, friendships. There are the saints of every day, the "hidden" saints, a sort of "middle class of holiness," as a French author said, that "middle class of holiness" to which we can all belong. But in different parts of the world, there are also those who suffer, like Peter and the Apostles, on account of the Gospel; there are those who give their lives in order to remain faithful to Christ by means of a witness marked by the shedding of their blood.

Let us all remember this: one cannot proclaim the Gospel of Jesus without the tangible witness of one's life. Those who listen to us and observe us must be able to see in our actions what they hear from our lips, and so give glory to God! I am thinking now of some advice that St. Francis of Assisi gave his brothers: preach the Gospel and, if necessary, use words. Preaching with your life, with your witness. Inconsistency on the part of pastors and the faithful between what they say and what they do, between word and manner of life, is undermining the Church's credibility.

All this is possible only if we recognize Jesus Christ, because it is he who has called us, he who has invited us to travel his path, he who has chosen us. Proclamation and witness are only possible if we are close to him, just as Peter, John, and the other disciples in today's Gospel passage were gathered around the Risen Jesus; there is a daily closeness to him: they know very well who he is, they know him. The Evangelist stresses the fact that no one "dared ask him: 'Who are you?' They knew it was the Lord" (Jn 21:12). And this is important for us: living an intense relationship with Jesus, an intimacy of dialogue and of life, in such a way as to recognize him as "the Lord." Worshipping him! The passage that we heard from the Book of Revelation speaks to us of worship: the myriads of angels, all creatures, the living beings, the elders, prostrate themselves before the Throne of God and of the Lamb that was slain, namely Christ, to whom be praise, honor, and glory (cf. Rev 5:11–14).

I would like all of us to ask ourselves this question: You, I, do we worship the Lord? Do we turn to God only to ask him for things, to thank him, or do we also turn to him to worship him? What does it mean, then, to worship God? It means learning to be with him, it means that we stop trying to dialogue with him, and it means sensing that his presence is the most true, the most good, the most important thing of all. All of us, in our own lives, consciously, and perhaps sometimes unconsciously, have a very clear order of priority concerning the things we consider important. Worshipping the Lord means giving him the place that he must have; worshipping the Lord means stating, believing — not only by our words — that he alone truly guides our lives; worshipping the Lord means that we are convinced before him that he is the only God, the God of our lives, the God of our history.

This has a consequence in our lives: we have to empty ourselves of the many small or great idols that we have and in which we take refuge, on which we often seek to base our security. They are idols that we sometimes keep well hidden; they can be ambition, careerism, a taste for success, placing ourselves at the center, the tendency to dominate others, the claim to be the sole masters of our lives, some sins to which we are bound, and many others. This evening I would like a question to resound in the heart of each one of you, and I would like you to answer it honestly: Have I considered which idol lies hidden in my life that prevents me from worshipping the Lord? Worshipping is stripping ourselves of our idols, even the most hidden ones, and choosing the Lord as the center, as the highway of our lives.

> Worshipping is stripping ourselves of our idols, even the most hidden ones, and choosing the Lord as the center, as the highway of our lives.

Dear brothers and sisters, each day the Lord calls us to follow him with courage and fidelity; he has made us the great gift of choosing us as his disciples; he invites us to proclaim him with joy as the Risen One, but he asks us to do so by word and by the witness of our lives, in daily life. The Lord is the only God of our lives, and he invites us to strip ourselves of our many idols and to worship him alone. To proclaim, to witness, to adore. May the Blessed Virgin Mary and St. Paul help us on this journey and intercede for us. Amen.

# Chapter Thirteen

## GENERAL AUDIENCE,[1] WEDNESDAY OF THE THIRD WEEK OF EASTER

In the Creed, we say that Jesus "ascended into heaven and is seated at the right hand of the Father." Jesus' earthly life culminated with the Ascension, when he passed from this world to the Father and was raised to sit on his right. What does this event mean? How does it affect our lives? What does contemplating Jesus seated at the right hand of the Father mean? Let us permit the Evangelist Luke to guide us in this.

Let us start from the moment when Jesus decided to make his last pilgrimage to Jerusalem. St. Luke notes: "When the days drew near for him to be received up, he set his face to go to Jerusalem" (Lk 9:51). While he was "going up" to the Holy City, where his own "exodus" from this life was to occur, Jesus already saw the destination, heaven, but he knew well that the way that would lead him to the glory of the Father passed through the Cross, through obedience to the divine design of love for mankind. The *Catechism of the Catholic Church* states that: "The lifting up of Jesus on the cross signifies and announces his lifting up by his Ascension into heaven" (n. 662).

---

1. April 17, 2013; St. Peter's Square.

We, too, should be clear in our Christian life that entering the glory of God demands daily fidelity to his will, even when it demands sacrifice, and sometimes requires us to change our plans. The Ascension of Jesus actually happened on the Mount of Olives, close to the place where he had withdrawn to pray before the Passion in order to remain in deep union with the Father: once again we see that prayer gives us the grace to be faithful to God's plan.

At the end of his Gospel, St. Luke gives a very concise account of the event of the Ascension. Jesus led his disciples "out as far as Bethany, and lifting up his hands he blessed them. While he blessed them, he parted from them, and was carried up into heaven. And they worshipped him, and returned to Jerusalem with great joy, and were continually in the temple blessing God" (Lk 24:50–53). This is what St. Luke says.

I would like to note two elements in the account. First of all, during the Ascension Jesus made the priestly gesture of blessing, and the disciples certainly expressed their faith with prostration, they knelt with bowed heads. This is a first important point: Jesus is the one eternal High Priest, who with his Passion passed through death and the tomb and ascended into heaven. He is with God the Father where he intercedes forever in our favor (cf. Heb 9:24). As St. John says in his First Letter, he is our Advocate: How beautiful it is to hear this! When someone is summoned by the judge or is involved in legal proceedings, the first thing he does is to seek a lawyer to defend him. We have One who always defends us, who defends us from the snares of the devil, who defends us from ourselves and from our sins!

Dear brothers and sisters, we have this Advocate; let us not be afraid to turn to him to ask forgiveness, to ask for a blessing, to ask for mercy! He always pardons us, he is our Advocate: he always defends us! Don't forget this! The Ascension of Jesus into heaven acquaints us with this deeply consoling reality on our journey: in Christ, true God and true man, our humanity was taken to God. Christ opened the path to us. He is like a roped guide climbing a mountain who, on reaching the summit, pulls us up to him and leads us to God. If we entrust our life to him, if we let ourselves be guided by him, we are certain to be in safe hands, in the hands of our Savior, of our Advocate.

A second element: St. Luke says that having seen Jesus ascending into heaven, the Apostles returned to Jerusalem "with great joy." This seems to us a little odd. When we are separated from our relatives, from our friends, because of a definitive departure and, especially, death, there is usually a natural sadness in us since we will no longer see their face, no longer hear their voice, or enjoy their love, their presence. The Evangelist instead emphasizes the profound joy of the Apostles.

But how could this be? Precisely because, with the gaze of faith, they understand that although he has been removed from their sight, Jesus stays with them forever, he does not abandon them, and in the glory of the Father supports them, guides them, and intercedes for them.

St. Luke, too, recounts the event of the Ascension — at the beginning of the Acts of the Apostles — to emphasize that this event is like the link of the chain that connects Jesus' earthly life to the life of the Church. Here, St. Luke also speaks of the cloud that hid Jesus from the sight of the disciples, who stood gazing at him ascending to God (cf. Acts 1:9–10). Then two men in white robes appeared and asked them not to stand there looking up to heaven, but to nourish their lives and their witness with the certainty that Jesus will come again in the same way in which they saw him ascending into heaven (cf. Acts 1:10–11). This is the invitation to base our contemplation on Christ's lordship, to find in him the strength to spread the Gospel, and to witness to it in everyday life: contemplation and action, *ora et labora*, as St. Benedict taught, are both necessary in our life as Christians.

> We are never alone: the Crucified and Risen Lord guides us.

Dear brothers and sisters, the Ascension does not point to Jesus' absence, but tells us that he is alive in our midst in a new way. He is no longer in a specific place in the world as he was before the Ascension. He is now in the lordship of God, present in every space and time, close to each one of us. In our life we are never alone: we have this Advocate who awaits us, who defends us. We are never alone: the Crucified and Risen Lord guides us. We have with us a multitude of brothers and sisters who, in silence and concealment, in their family life and at work, in their problems and hardships, in their joys and hopes, live faith daily, and together with us bring the world the lordship of God's love, in the Risen Jesus Christ, ascended into heaven, our own Advocate who pleads for us. Many thanks.

# Chapter Fourteen

# *REGINA CAELI* ADDRESS,[1]
# FOURTH SUNDAY OF EASTER

T
he Fourth Sunday of the Season of Easter is characterized by the Gospel of the Good Shepherd in chapter ten of St. John, which is read every year. Today's passage records these words of Jesus: "My sheep hear my voice, and I know them, and they follow me; and I give them eternal life, and they shall never perish, and no one shall snatch them out of my hand. My Father, who has given them to me, is greater than all, and no one is able to snatch them out of the Father's hand. I and the Father are one" (10:27–30). These four verses contain the whole of Jesus' message; it is the nucleus of his Gospel: he calls us to share in his relationship with the Father, and this is eternal life.

Jesus wants to establish with his friends a relationship that mirrors his own relationship with the Father: a relationship of reciprocal belonging in full trust, in intimate communion. To express this profound understanding, this relationship of friendship, Jesus uses the image of the shepherd with his sheep: he calls them and they recognize his voice, they respond to his call and follow him. This parable is very beautiful! The mystery of

---

1. April 21, 2013; St. Peter's Square.

his voice is evocative: only think that from our mother's womb we learn to recognize her voice and that of our father; it is from the tone of a voice that we perceive love or contempt, affection or coldness. Jesus' voice is unique! If we learn to distinguish it, he guides us on the path of life, a path that goes beyond even the abyss of death.

However, Jesus, at a certain point, said: "my Father, who has given them to me ..." (Jn 10:29), referring to his sheep. This is very important, it is a profound mystery, far from easy to understand. If I feel drawn to Jesus, if his voice warms my heart, it is thanks to God the Father who has sown within me the desire for love, for truth, for life, for beauty ... and Jesus is all this in fullness! This helps us understand the mystery of vocation and especially of the call to a special consecration. Sometimes Jesus calls us, he invites us to follow him, but perhaps we do not realize that it is he who is calling, like what happened to the young Samuel. There are many young people today, here in the Square. There are large numbers of you aren't there? It's clear.... Look! Here in the Square today there are so many of you! I would like to ask you: have you sometimes heard the Lord's voice, in a desire, in a worry, did he invite you to follow him more closely? Have you heard him? I can't hear you? There! Have you wanted to be apostles of Jesus? We must bet on youth for the great ideals. Do you think this? Do you agree? Ask Jesus what he wants of you and be brave! Be brave! Ask him this!

> Ask Jesus what he wants of you and be brave! Be brave! Ask him this!

Behind and before every vocation to the priesthood or to the consecrated life, there is always the strong and intense prayer of someone: a grandmother, a grandfather, a mother, a father, a community…. This is why Jesus said: "Pray therefore the Lord of the harvest," that is, God the Father, "to send out laborers into his harvest" (Mt 9:38). Vocations are born in prayer and from prayer; and only through prayer can they persevere and bear fruit. I am pleased to stress this today, which is the "World Day of Prayer for Vocations."

Let us pray in particular for the new priests of the Diocese of Rome whom I have had the joy to ordain. And let us invoke the intercession of Mary. There were ten young men who said "yes" to Jesus and they have been ordained priests. This is beautiful!

Let us invoke the intercession of Mary who is the Woman of the "yes." Mary said yes throughout her life! She learned to recognize Jesus' voice from the time when she carried him in her womb. May Mary, our Mother, help us to know Jesus' voice better and better, and to follow it, so as to walk on the path of life! Thank you.

Thank you so much for your greeting, but greet Jesus too. Shout "Jesus" very loudly…. Let us all pray together to Our Lady.

## Chapter Fifteen

# HOMILY,[1]
# TUESDAY OF THE FOURTH WEEK
# OF EASTER

Today's first reading makes me think that, at the very moment when persecution broke out, the Church's missionary nature also "broke out." These Christians went all the way to Phoenicia, Cyprus, and Antioch, and proclaimed the Word (cf. Acts 11:19). They had this apostolic fervor in their hearts; and so the faith spread! Some people from Cyprus and Cyrene, not these but others who had become Christians, came to Antioch and began to speak also to the Greeks (cf. Acts 11:20). This is yet another step. And so the Church moves forward. Who took this initiative of speaking to the Greeks, something unheard of, since they were preaching only to Jews? It was the Holy Spirit, the one who was pushing them on, on, and on, unceasingly.

But back in Jerusalem, when somebody heard about this, he got a little nervous, and they sent an *Apostolic Visitation*: they sent Barnabas (cf. Acts 11:22). Perhaps, with a touch of humor, we can say that this was the theological origin of the Congregation for the Doctrine of the Faith: this *Apostolic Visitation* of Barnabas. He took a

---

1. Feast of St. George; April 23, 2013; Pauline Chapel.

look and saw that things were going well (cf. Acts 11:23). And in this way the Church is increasingly a Mother, a Mother of many, many children: she becomes a Mother, ever more fully a Mother, a Mother who gives us faith, a Mother who gives us our identity. But Christian identity is not an identity card. Christian identity means being a member of the Church, since all these people belonged to the Church, to Mother Church, for apart from the Church it is not possible to find Jesus. The great Pope Paul VI said: it is an absurd dichotomy to wish to live with Jesus but without the Church, to follow Jesus but without the Church, to love Jesus but without the Church (cf. *Evangelii Nuntiandi*, 16). And that Mother Church who gives us Jesus also gives us an identity that is not simply a rubber stamp: it is membership. Identity means membership, belonging. Belonging to the Church: this is beautiful!

The third idea that comes to my mind — the first was the outbreak of the Church's missionary nature, and the second, the Church as Mother — is that, when Barnabas saw that crowd — the text says: "and a great many people were brought to the Lord" (Acts 11:24) — when he saw that crowd, he rejoiced. "When he came and saw the grace of God, he rejoiced" (Acts 11:23). It is the special joy of the evangelizer. It is, as Pope Paul VI said, "the delightful and comforting joy of evangelizing" (cf. *Evangelii Nuntiandi*, 80). This joy begins with persecution, with great sadness, and ends in joy. And so the Church moves forward, as a Saint tells us, amid the persecutions of the world and the consolations of the Lord (cf. St. Augustine,

*De Civitate Dei*, 18:51, 2: PL 41, 614). This is the life of the Church. If we want to take the path of worldliness, bargaining with the world — as the Maccabeans were tempted to do back then — we will never have the consolation of the Lord. And if we seek consolation alone, it will be a superficial consolation, not the Lord's consolation, but a human consolation. The Church always advances between the Cross and the Resurrection, between persecutions and the consolations of the Lord. This is the path: those who take this path do not go wrong.

Today let us think about the missionary nature of the Church: these disciples who took the initiative to go forth,

> The Church always advances between the Cross and the Resurrection, between persecutions and the consolations of the Lord.

and those who had the courage to proclaim Jesus to the Greeks, something that at that time was almost scandalous (cf. Acts 11:19–20). Let us think of Mother Church, who is increasing, growing with new children to whom she gives the identity of faith, for one cannot believe in Jesus without the Church. Jesus himself says so in the Gospel: but you do not believe because you do not belong to my sheep (cf. Jn 10:26). Unless we are "Jesus' sheep," faith does not come; it is a faith that is watered down, insubstantial. And let us think of the consolation that Barnabas experienced, which was precisely the "delightful and comforting joy of evangelizing." Let us ask the Lord for this *parrhesia*, this apostolic fervor that impels us to move forward, as brothers and sisters, all of

us: forward! Forward, bearing the name of Jesus in the
bosom of Holy Mother Church, as St. Ignatius said, hi-
erarchical and Catholic. Amen.

# Chapter Sixteen

# General Audience,[1] Wednesday of the Fourth Week of Easter

In the Creed we profess that Jesus "will come again in glory to judge the living and the dead." Human history begins with the creation of man and woman in God's likeness and ends with the Last Judgment of Christ. These two poles of history are often forgotten; and, at times, especially faith in Christ's return and in the Last Judgment are not so clear and firm in Christian hearts. In his public life, Jesus frequently reflected on the reality of his Final Coming. Today I would like to reflect on three Gospel texts that help us to penetrate this mystery: those of the ten virgins, of the talents, and of the Last Judgment. All three are part of Jesus' discourse on the end of time, which can be found in the Gospel of St. Matthew.

Let us remember first of all that in the Ascension the Son of God brought to the Father our humanity, which he had taken on, and that he wants to draw all to himself, to call the whole world to be welcomed in God's embrace so that at the end of history the whole of reality may be consigned to the Father. Yet there is

---

1. April 24, 2013; St. Peter's Square.

this "immediate time" between the First and the Final Coming of Christ, and that is the very time in which we are living. The parable of the ten virgins fits into this context of "immediate" time (cf. Mt 25:1–13). They are ten maidens who are awaiting the arrival of the Bridegroom, but he is late, and they fall asleep. At the sudden announcement that the Bridegroom is arriving they prepare to welcome him, but while five of them, who are wise, have oil to burn in their lamps, the others, who are foolish, are left with lamps that have gone out because they have no oil for them. While they go to get some oil, the Bridegroom arrives and the foolish virgins find that the door to the hall of the marriage feast is shut.

They knock on it again and again, but it is now too late, the Bridegroom answers: I do not know you. The Bridegroom is the Lord, and the time of waiting for his arrival is the time he gives to us, to all of us, before his Final Coming with mercy and patience; it is a time of watchfulness; a time in which we must keep alight the lamps of faith, hope, and charity, a time in which to keep our heart open to goodness, beauty, and truth. It is a time to live in accordance with God, because we do not know either the day or the hour of Christ's return. What he asks of us is to be ready for the encounter — ready for an encounter, for a beautiful encounter, the encounter with Jesus, which means being able to see the signs of his presence, keeping our faith alive with prayer, with the sacraments, and taking care not to fall asleep so as to not forget about God. The life of slumbering Christians is a sad life, it is not a happy life. Christians must be happy, with the joy of Jesus. Let us not fall asleep!

The second parable, the parable of the talents, makes us think about the relationship between how we use the gifts we have received from God and his return, when he will ask us what use we made of them (cf. Mt 25:14–30). We are well acquainted with the parable: before his departure the master gives a few talents to each of his servants to ensure that they will be put to good use during his absence. He gives five to the first servant, two to the second one, and one to the third. In the period of their master's absence, the first two servants increase their talents — these are ancient coins — whereas the third servant prefers to bury his and to return it to his master as it was.

On his return, the master judges what they have done: he praises the first two while he throws the third one out into the outer darkness because, through fear, he had hidden his talent, withdrawing into himself. A Christian who withdraws into himself, who hides everything that the Lord has given him, is a Christian who … he is not a Christian! He is a Christian who does not thank God for everything God has given him!

This tells us that the expectation of the Lord's return is the time of action — we are in the time of action — the time in which we should bring God's gifts to fruition, not for ourselves but for him, for the Church, for others. The time to seek to increase goodness in the world always; and in particular, in this period of crisis, today, it is important not to turn in on ourselves, burying our own talent, our spiritual, intellectual, and material riches, everything that the Lord has given us, but, rather to open ourselves, to be supportive, to be attentive to others.

In the square I have seen that there are many young people here: it is true, isn't it? Are there many young people? Where are they? I ask you who are just setting out on your journey through life: have you thought about the talents that God has given you? Have you thought of how you can put them at the service of others? Do not bury your talents! Set your stakes on great ideals, the ideals that enlarge the heart, the ideals of service that make your talents fruitful. Life is not given to us to be jealously guarded for ourselves, but is given to us so that we may give it in turn. Dear young people, have a deep spirit! Do not be afraid to dream of great things!

Lastly, a word about the passage on the Last Judgment in which the Lord's Second Coming is described, when he will judge all human beings, the living and the dead (cf. Mt 25: 31–46). The image used by the Evangelist is that of the shepherd who separates the sheep from the goats. On his right he places those who have acted in accordance with God's will, who went to the aid of their hungry, thirsty, foreign, naked, sick, or imprisoned neighbor — I said "foreign": I am thinking of the multitude of foreigners who are here in the Diocese of Rome: what do we do for them? While on his left are those who did not help their neighbor. This tells us that God will judge us on our love, on how we have loved our brethren, especially the weakest and the neediest. Of course we must always have clearly in mind that we are justified, we are saved through grace, through an act of freely given love by God, who always goes before us; on our own we can do nothing. Faith is first of all a gift we have received. But in order to bear fruit, God's grace always demands our openness to him, our free and tangible response. Christ comes to bring us the mercy of a God who saves. We are asked to trust in him, to correspond to the gift of his love with a good life, made up of actions motivated by faith and love.

> Christ comes to bring us the mercy of a God who saves.

Dear brothers and sisters, may looking at the Last Judgment never frighten us: rather, may it impel us to live the present better. God offers us this time with mercy and patience so that we may learn every day to recognize him in the poor and in the lowly. Let us strive for goodness and be watchful in prayer and in love. May the Lord, at the end of our life and at the end of history, be able to recognize us as good and faithful servants. Many thanks!

# Chapter Seventeen

# HOMILY,[1]
## FIFTH SUNDAY OF EASTER

I would like to offer three short and simple thoughts for your reflection.

To begin: In the second reading, we listened to the beautiful vision of St. John: new heavens and a new earth, and then the Holy City coming down from God. All is new, changed into good, beauty, and truth; there are no more tears or mourning.... This is the work of the Holy Spirit: he brings us the new things of God. He comes to us and makes all things new; he changes us. The Spirit changes us! And St. John's vision reminds us that all of us are journeying toward the heavenly Jerusalem, the ultimate newness, which awaits us and all reality, the happy day when we will see the Lord's face — that marvelous face, the most beautiful face of the Lord Jesus — and be with him forever, in his love.

You see, the new things of God are not like the novelties of this world, all of which are temporary; they come and go, and we keep looking for more. The new things that God gives to our lives are lasting, not only in the future, when we will be with him, but today as well. God is

1. Holy Mass and Conferral of the Sacrament of Confirmation; April 28, 2013; St. Peter's Square.

even now making all things new; the Holy Spirit is truly transforming us, and through us he also wants to transform the world in which we live. Let us open the doors to the Spirit, let ourselves be guided by him, and allow God's constant help to make us new men and women, inspired by the love of God that the Holy Spirit bestows on us! How beautiful it would be if each of you, every evening, could say: Today at school, at home, at work, guided by God, I showed a sign of love toward one of my friends, my parents, an older person! How beautiful!

A second thought. In the first reading, Paul and Barnabas say that "we must undergo many trials if we are to enter the kingdom of God" (Acts 14:22). The journey of the Church, and our own personal journeys as Christians, are not always easy; they meet with difficulties and trials. To follow the Lord, to let his Spirit transform the shadowy parts of our lives, our ungodly ways of acting, and cleanse us of our sins, is to set out on a path with many obstacles, both in the world around us but also within us, in the heart. But difficulties and trials are part of the path that leads to God's glory, just as they were for Jesus, who was glorified on the Cross; we will always encounter them in life! Do not be discouraged! We have the power of the Holy Spirit to overcome these trials!

And here I come to my last point. It is an invitation, which I make to you, young confirmandi, and to all present. Remain steadfast in the journey of faith, with firm hope in the Lord. This is the secret of our journey! He gives us the courage to swim against the tide. Pay attention, my young friends: to go against the current; this is good for the heart, but we need courage to swim against the tide. Jesus gives us this courage! There are no difficulties, trials, or misunderstandings to fear, provided we remain united to God as branches to the vine, provided we do not lose our friendship with him, provided we make ever more room for him in our lives. This is especially so whenever we feel poor, weak, and sinful, because God

> Remain steadfast in the journey of faith, with firm hope in the Lord. This is the secret of our journey! He gives us the courage to swim against the tide.

grants strength to our weakness, riches to our poverty, conversion and forgiveness to our sinfulness. The Lord is so rich in mercy: every time, if we go to him, he forgives us. Let us trust in God's work! With him we can do great things; he will give us the joy of being his disciples, his witnesses. Commit yourselves to great ideals, to the most important things. We Christians were not chosen by the Lord for little things; push onward toward the highest principles. Stake your lives on noble ideals, my dear young people!

The new things of God, the trials of life, remaining steadfast in the Lord. Dear friends, let us open wide the door of our lives to the new things of God that the Holy Spirit gives us. May he transform us, confirm us in our trials, strengthen our union with the Lord, our steadfastness in him: this is a true joy! So may it be.

# Chapter Eighteen

# HOMILY,[1]
# SIXTH SUNDAY OF EASTER

As part of the journey of the Year of Faith, I am happy to celebrate this Eucharist dedicated in a special way to confraternities: a traditional reality in the Church, which in recent times has experienced renewal and rediscovery. I greet all of you with affection, particularly the confraternities that have come here from all over the world! Thank you for your presence and your witness!

In the Gospel we heard a passage from the farewell discourses of Jesus, as related by the Evangelist John in the context of the Last Supper. Jesus entrusts his last thoughts, as a spiritual testament, to the Apostles before he leaves them. Today's text makes it clear that Christian faith is completely centered on the relationship between the Father, the Son, and the Holy Spirit. Whoever loves the Lord Jesus welcomes him and his Father interiorly, and, thanks to the Holy Spirit, receives the Gospel in his or her heart and life. Here we are shown the center from which everything must go forth and to which everything

1. Holy Mass on the Occasion of the Day of Confraternities and Popular Piety; May 5, 2013; St. Peter's Square.

must lead: loving God and being Christ's disciples by living the Gospel.

When Pope Benedict XVI spoke to you, he used this expression: evangelical spirit. Dear confraternities, the popular piety of which you are an important sign is a treasure possessed by the Church, which the bishops of Latin America defined, significantly, as a spirituality, a form of mysticism, which is "a place of encounter with Jesus Christ." Draw always from Christ, the inexhaustible wellspring; strengthen your faith by attending to your spiritual formation, to personal and communitarian prayer, and to the liturgy. Down the centuries confraternities have been crucibles of holiness for countless people who have lived in utter simplicity an intense relationship with the Lord. Advance with determination along the path of holiness; do not rest content with a mediocre Christian life, but let your affiliation serve as a stimulus, above all for you yourselves, to an ever greater love of Jesus Christ.

The passage of the Acts of the Apostles that we heard also speaks to us about what is essential. In the early Church there was immediately a need to discern what was essential about being a Christian, about following Christ, and what was not. The Apostles and the other elders held an important meeting in Jerusalem, a first "council," on this theme, to discuss the problems that arose after the Gospel had been preached to the pagans, to non-Jews. It was a providential opportunity for better understanding what is essential, namely, belief in Jesus Christ who died and rose for our sins, and loving him as he loved us. But note how the difficulties were overcome: not from without, but from within the Church. And this brings up a second element that I want to remind you of, as Pope Benedict XVI did, namely: ecclesial spirit. Popular piety is a road that leads to what is essential if it is lived in the Church in profound communion with your pastors.

Dear brothers and sisters, the Church loves you! Be an active presence in the community, as living cells, as living stones. The Latin American bishops wrote that the popular piety that you reflect is "a legitimate way of living the faith, a way of feeling that we are part of the Church" (*Aparecida Document*, 264). This is wonderful! A legitimate way of living the faith, a way of feeling that we are part of the Church. Love the Church! Let yourselves be guided by her! In your parishes, in your dioceses, be a true "lung" of faith and Christian life, a breath of fresh air! In this Square, I see a great variety: earlier on it was a variety of umbrellas, and now of colors and signs. This is also the case with the Church: a great wealth and variety of expressions in which everything leads back to unity; the variety leads back to unity, and unity is the encounter with Christ.

I would like to add a third expression that must distinguish you: missionary spirit. You have a specific and important mission, that of keeping alive the relationship between the faith and the cultures of the peoples to whom you belong. You do this through popular piety. When, for example, you carry the crucifix in procession with such great veneration and love for the Lord, you are not performing a simple outward act; you are pointing to the centrality of the Lord's paschal mystery, his Passion, death, and Resurrection, which have redeemed us, and you are reminding yourselves first, as well as the community, that we have to follow Christ along the concrete path of our daily lives so that he can transform us. Likewise, when you express profound devotion for the Virgin Mary, you are pointing to the highest realization of the Christian life, the one who by her faith and obedience to God's will, and by her meditation on the words and deeds of Jesus, is the Lord's perfect disciple (cf. *Lumen Gentium*, 53).

You express this faith, born of hearing the word of God, in ways that engage the senses, the emotions, and the symbols of the different cultures.... In doing so you help to transmit it to others, and especially the simple persons whom, in the Gospels, Jesus calls "the little ones." In effect, "journeying together toward shrines, and participating in other demonstrations of popular piety, bringing along your children and engaging other people, is itself a work of evangelization" (*Aparecida Document*, 264). When you visit shrines, when you bring your family, your children, you are engaged in a real work of evangelization. This needs to continue.

May you also be true evangelizers! May your initiatives be "bridges," means of bringing others to Christ, so as to journey together with him. And in this spirit may you always be attentive to charity. Each individual Christian and every community is missionary to the extent that they bring to others and live the Gospel, and testify to God's love for all, especially those experiencing difficulties. Be missionaries of God's love and tenderness! Be missionaries of God's mercy, which always forgives us, always awaits us, and loves us dearly.

Evangelical spirit, ecclesial spirit, missionary spirit. Three themes! Do not forget them! Evangelical spirit, ecclesial spirit, missionary spirit. Let us ask the Lord always to direct our minds and hearts to him, as living stones of the Church, so that all that we do, our whole Christian life, may be a luminous witness to his mercy and love. In this way we will make our way toward the goal of our earthly pilgrimage, toward that extremely beautiful shrine, the heavenly Jerusalem. There, there is no longer any temple: God himself and the lamb are its temple; and the light of the sun and the moon give way to the glory of the Most High. Amen.

Be missionaries of God's love and tenderness! Be missionaries of God's mercy, which always forgives us, always awaits us, and loves us dearly.

# Chapter Nineteen

# GENERAL AUDIENCE,[1]
# WEDNESDAY OF THE SIXTH WEEK
# OF EASTER

The Easter Season that we are living joyfully, guided by the Church's liturgy, is *par excellence* the season of the Holy Spirit given "without measure" (cf. Jn 3:34) by Jesus Crucified and Risen. This time of grace closes with the Feast of Pentecost, in which the Church relives the outpouring of the Spirit upon Mary and the Apostles gathered in prayer in the Upper Room.

But who is the Holy Spirit? In the Creed, we profess with faith: "I believe in the Holy Spirit, the Lord and Giver of life." The first truth to which we adhere in the Creed is that the Holy Spirit is *Kýrios*, Lord. This signifies that he is truly God, just as the Father and the Son are; the object, on our part, of the same act of adoration and glorification that we address to the Father and to the Son. Indeed, the Holy Spirit is the Third Person of the Most Holy Trinity; he is the great gift of Christ Risen who opens our mind and our heart to faith in Jesus as the Son sent by the Father and who leads us to friendship, to communion with God.

---

1. May 8, 2013; St. Peter's Square.

However, I would like to focus especially on the fact that *the Holy Spirit is the inexhaustible source of God's life in us*. Man of every time and place desires a full and beautiful life, just and good, a life that is not threatened by death, but can still mature and grow to fullness. Man is like a traveler who, crossing the deserts of life, thirsts for the living water: gushing and fresh, capable of quenching his deep desire for light, love, beauty, and peace. We all feel this desire! And Jesus gives us this living water: he is the Holy Spirit, who proceeds from the Father and whom Jesus pours out into our hearts. "I came that they may have life, and have it abundantly," Jesus tells us (Jn 10:10).

Jesus promised the Samaritan woman that he will give a superabundance of "living water" forever to all those who recognize him as the Son sent by the Father to save us (cf. Jn 4:5–26; 3:17). Jesus came to give us this "living water," who is the Holy Spirit, that our life might be guided by God, might be moved by God, nourished by God. When we say that a Christian is a spiritual being, we mean just this: the Christian is a person who thinks and acts in accordance with God, in accordance with the Holy Spirit. But I ask myself: and do we, do we think in accordance with God? Do we act in accordance with God? Or do we let ourselves be guided by the many other things that certainly do not come from God? Each one of us needs to respond to this in the depths of his or her own heart.

At this point we may ask ourselves: why can this water quench our thirst deep down? We know that water is

essential to life; without water we die; it quenches, washes, makes the earth fertile. In the Letter to the Romans
we find these words: "God's love has been poured into
our hearts through the Holy Spirit who has been given to
us" (5:5). The "living water," the Holy Spirit, the Gift of
the Risen One who dwells in us, purifies us, illuminates
us, renews us, transforms us because he makes us partici-
pants in the very life of God who is Love. That is why the
Apostle Paul says that the Christian's life is moved by the
Holy Spirit and by his fruit, which is "love, joy, peace,
patience, kindness, goodness, faithfulness, gentleness,
self-control" (Gal 5:22–23). *The Holy Spirit introduces us
to divine life as "children in the Only Begotten Son."*

In another passage from the Letter to the Romans,
which we have recalled several times, St. Paul sums it up
with these words: "For all who are led by the Spirit of
God are sons of God. For you ... have received the spirit
of sonship. When we cry, 'Abba! Father!' it is the Spirit
himself bearing witness with our spirit that we are children of God, and if children, then heirs, heirs of God and
fellow heirs with Christ, provided we suffer with him in
order that we may also be glorified with him" (8:14–17).
This is the precious gift that the Holy Spirit brings to our
hearts: the very life of God, the life of true children, a
relationship of confidence, freedom, and trust in the love
and mercy of God. It also gives us a new perception of
others, close and far, seen always as brothers and sisters
in Jesus to be respected and loved.

The Holy Spirit teaches us to see with the eyes of
Christ, to live life as Christ lived, to understand life as

Christ understood it. That is why the living water, who is the Holy Spirit, quenches our life, why he tells us that we are loved by God as children, that we can love God as his children, and that by his grace we can live as children of God, like Jesus. And we, do we listen to the Holy Spirit? What does the Holy Spirit tell us? He says: God loves you. He tells us this. God loves you, God likes you. Do we truly love God and others, as Jesus does? Let us allow ourselves to be guided by the Holy Spirit, let us allow him to speak to our heart and say this to us: God is love, God is waiting for us, God is Father, he loves us as a true father loves, he loves us truly, and only the Holy Spirit can tell us this in our hearts. Let us hear the Holy Spirit, let us listen to the Holy Spirit, and may we move forward on this path of love, mercy, and forgiveness. Thank you.

> What does the Holy Spirit tell us? He says: God loves you. He tells us this. God loves you, God likes you.

# Chapter Twenty

# HOMILY,[1]
## SEVENTH SUNDAY OF EASTER

On this Seventh Sunday of Easter, we gather together in joy to celebrate a feast of holiness. Let us give thanks to God who made his glory, the glory of Love, shine on the Martyrs of Otranto, on Mother Laura Montoya, and on Mother María Guadalupe García Zavala. I greet all who have come for this celebration — from Italy, Colombia, Mexico, and other countries — and I thank you! Let us look at the new saints in the light of the word of God proclaimed. It is a word that has invited us to be faithful to Christ, even to martyrdom; it has reminded us of the urgency and beauty of bringing Christ and his Gospel to everyone; and it has spoken to us of the testimony of charity, without which even martyrdom and the mission lose their Christian savor.

When the Acts of the Apostles tell us about the Deacon Stephen, the Proto-Martyr, it is written that he was a man "filled with the Holy Spirit" (6:5; 7:55). What does this mean? It means that he was filled with the Love of God, that his whole self, his life, was inspired by the

---

1. Holy Mass and Canonizations; May 12, 2013; St. Peter's Square.

Spirit of the Risen Christ so that he followed Jesus with total fidelity, to the point of giving up himself.

Today the Church holds up for our veneration an array of martyrs who in 1480 were called to bear the highest witness to the Gospel together. About 800 people who had survived the siege and invasion of Otranto were beheaded in the environs of that city. They refused to deny their faith and died professing the Risen Christ. Where did they find the strength to stay faithful? In the faith itself, which enables us to see beyond the limits of our human sight, beyond the boundaries of earthly life. It grants us to contemplate "the heavens opened," as St. Stephen says, and the living Christ at God's right hand. Dear friends, let us keep the faith we have received, which is our true treasure; let us renew our faithfulness to the Lord, even in the midst of obstacles and misunderstanding. God will never let us lack strength and calmness. While we venerate the Martyrs of Otranto, let us ask God to sustain all the Christians who still suffer violence today in these very times and in so many parts of the world and to give them the courage to stay faithful and to respond to evil with goodness.

We might take the second idea from the words of Jesus that we heard in the Gospel: "I do not pray for these only, but also for those who believe in me through their word, that they may all be one; even as you, Father, are in me, and I in you, that they also may be in us" (Jn 17:20). St. Laura Montoya was an instrument of evangelization, first as a teacher and later as a spiritual mother of the indigenous in whom she instilled hope, welcoming them with this love that she had learned from God and bringing them to him with an effective pedagogy that respected their culture and was not in opposition to it. In her work of evangelization, Mother Laura truly made herself all things to all people, to borrow St. Paul's words (cf. 1 Cor 9:22). Today, too, like a vanguard of the Church, her spiritual daughters live in and take the Gospel to the farthest and most needy places.

This first saint, born in the beautiful country of Colombia, teaches us to be generous to God and not to live our faith in solitude — as if it were possible to live the faith alone! — but to communicate it and to make the joy of the Gospel shine out in our words and in the witness of our life wherever we meet others. Wherever we may happen to be, to radiate this life of the Gospel. She teaches us to see Jesus' face reflected in others and to get the better of the indifference and individualism that corrode Christian communities and eat away our heart itself. She also teaches us to accept everyone without prejudice, without discrimination, and without reticence, but rather with sincere love, giving them the very best of ourselves and, especially, sharing with them our most worthwhile possession; this is not one of our institutions or organizations, no. The most worthwhile thing we possess is Christ and his Gospel.

Lastly, a third idea. In today's Gospel, Jesus prays to the Father with these words: "I made known to them your name, and I will make it known, that the love with which you have loved me may be in them, and I in them" (Jn 17:26). The martyr's fidelity, even to the death, and the proclamation of the Gospel to all people are rooted, have their roots, in God's love, which was poured out into our hearts by the Holy Spirit (cf. Rom 5:5), and in the witness we must bear in our life to this love.

The poor, the abandoned, the sick, and the marginalized are the flesh of Christ.

St. Guadalupe García Zavala was well aware of this. By renouncing a comfortable life — what great harm an easy life and well-being cause; the adoption of a bourgeois heart paralyzes us — by renouncing an easy life in order to follow Jesus' call, she taught people how to love poverty, how to feel greater love for the poor and for the sick. Mother Lupita would kneel on the hospital floor, before the sick, before the abandoned, in order to serve them with tenderness and compassion. And this is called "touching the flesh of Christ." The poor, the abandoned, the sick, and the marginalized are the flesh of Christ. And Mother Lupita touched the flesh of Christ and taught us this behavior: not to feel ashamed, not to fear, not to find "touching Christ's flesh" repugnant. Mother Lupita had realized what "touching Christ's flesh" actually means. Today, too, her spiritual daughters try to mirror God's love in works of charity, unsparing in sacrifices and facing every obstacle with docility and with apostolic perseverance (*hypomonē*), bearing it with courage.

This new Mexican saint invites us to love as Jesus loved us. This does not entail withdrawal into ourselves, into our own problems, into our own ideas, into our own interests, into this small world that is so harmful to us;

but rather to come out of ourselves and care for those who are in need of attention, understanding, and help, to bring them the warm closeness of God's love through tangible actions of sensitivity, of sincere affection, and of love.

Faithfulness to Christ and to his Gospel, in order to proclaim them with our words and our life, witnessing to God's love with our own love and with our charity to all: these are the luminous examples and teachings that the saints canonized today offer us, but they call into question our Christian life: how am I faithful to Christ? Let us take this question with us, to think about it during the day: how am I faithful to Christ? Am I able to "make my faith seen with respect, but also with courage"? Am I attentive to others, do I notice who is in need, do I see everyone as brothers and sisters to love? Let us ask the Lord, through the intercession of the Blessed Virgin Mary and the new saints, to fill our life with the joy of his love. So may it be.

# Chapter Twenty-One

## General Audience,[1] Wednesday of the Seventh Week of Easter

I would like to reflect on the Holy Spirit's action in guiding the Church and each one of us to the Truth. Jesus himself told his disciples: the Holy Spirit "will guide you into all the truth" (Jn 16:13), since he himself is "the Spirit of Truth" (cf. Jn 14:17; 15:26; 16:13).

We are living in an age in which people are rather skeptical of truth. Pope Benedict XVI has frequently spoken of relativism; that is, of the tendency to consider nothing definitive and to think that truth comes from consensus or from something we like. The question arises: does "the" truth really exist? What is "the" truth? Can we know it? Can we find it? Here springs to my mind the question of Pontius Pilate, the Roman Procurator, when Jesus reveals to him the deep meaning of his mission: "What is truth?" (Jn 18:37, 38). Pilate cannot understand that "the" Truth is standing in front of him, he cannot see in Jesus the face of the truth that is the face of God. And yet Jesus is exactly this: the Truth that, in the fullness of time, "became

---

1. May 15, 2013; St. Peter's Square.

flesh" (cf. Jn 1:1, 14) and came to dwell among us so that we might know it. The truth is not grasped as a thing, the truth is encountered. It is not a possession, it is an encounter with a Person.

But who can enable us to recognize that Jesus is "the" Word of truth, the Only Begotten Son of God the Father? St. Paul teaches that "no one can say 'Jesus is Lord' except by the Holy Spirit" (1 Cor 12:3). It is the Holy Spirit himself, the gift of the Risen Christ, who makes us recognize the Truth. Jesus describes him as the "Paraclete," namely, "the one who comes to our aid," who is beside us to sustain us on this journey of knowledge; and, at the Last Supper, Jesus assures the disciples that the Holy Spirit will teach them all things and remind them of all he has said to them (cf. Jn 14:26).

So how does the Holy Spirit act in our life and in the life of the Church in order to guide us to the truth? First of all, he recalls and impresses in the heart of believers the words Jesus spoke and, through these very words, the law of God — as the Prophets of the Old Testament had foretold — is engraved in our heart and becomes within us a criterion for evaluation in decisions and for guidance in our daily actions; it becomes a principle to live by. Ezekiel's great prophesy is brought about: "You shall be clean from all your uncleannesses, and from all your idols I will cleanse you. A new heart I will give you, and a new spirit I will put within you.… And I will put my spirit within you, and cause you to walk in my statutes and be careful to observe my ordinances" (Ezek 36:25–27). Indeed, it is in our inmost depths that our actions come into being: it is the heart itself that must be converted to God, and the Holy Spirit transforms it when we open ourselves to him.

Then, as Jesus promised, the Holy Spirit guides us "into all the truth" (Jn 16:13); not only does he guide us to the encounter with Jesus, the fullness of the Truth, but he also guides us "into" the Truth; that is, he makes us enter into an ever deeper communion with Jesus, giving us knowledge of all the things of God. And we cannot achieve this by our own efforts. Unless God enlightens us from within, our Christian existence will be superficial. The Church's Tradition asserts that the Spirit of truth acts in our heart, inspiring that "sense of the faith" (*sensus fidei*) through which, as the Second Vatican Council states, the People of God, under the guidance of the Magisterium, adheres unfailingly to the faith transmitted, penetrates it more deeply with the right judgment, and applies it more fully in life (cf. Dogmatic Constitution *Lumen Gentium*, n. 12). Let us try asking ourselves: am I open to the action of the Holy Spirit? Do I pray him to give me illumination, to make me more sensitive to God's things?

This is a prayer we must pray every day: "Holy Spirit, make my heart open to the word of God, make my heart open to goodness, make my heart open to the beauty of God every day." I would like to ask everyone a question: how many of you pray every day to the Holy Spirit? There will not be many, but we must fulfill Jesus' wish and pray every day to the Holy Spirit that he open our heart to Jesus.

Let us think of Mary, who "kept all these things, pondering them in her heart" (Lk 2:19, 51). Acceptance of the words and truth of faith, so that they may become life, is brought about and increases under the action of the Holy Spirit. In this regard, we must learn from Mary, we must relive her "yes," her unreserved readiness to receive the Son of God in her life, which was transformed from that moment. Through the Holy Spirit, the Father and the Son take up their abode with us: we live in God and of God. Yet, is our life truly inspired by God? How many things do I put before God?

Dear brothers and sisters, we need to let ourselves be bathed in the light of the Holy Spirit so that he may lead us into the Truth of God, who is the one Lord of our life. In this Year of Faith, let us ask ourselves whether we really have taken some steps to know Christ and the truth of faith better by reading and meditating on Sacred Scripture, by studying the *Catechism*, and by receiving the sacraments regularly. However, let us ask ourselves at the same time what steps we are taking to ensure that faith governs the whole of our existence. We are not Christian "part-time," only at certain moments, in certain circumstances, in certain decisions; no one can be Christian in this way, we are Christian all the time! Totally! May

> May Christ's truth, which the Holy Spirit teaches us and gives to us, always and totally affect our daily life.

Christ's truth, which the Holy Spirit teaches us and gives to us, always and totally affect our daily life. Let us call on him more often, so that he may guide us on the path of disciples of Christ. Let us call on him every day. I am making this suggestion to you: let us invoke the Holy Spirit every day, in this way the Holy Spirit will bring us close to Jesus Christ.

# Chapter Twenty-Two

# HOMILY,[1]
# PENTECOST SUNDAY

Let us contemplate and relive in the liturgy the outpouring of the Holy Spirit sent by the risen Christ
upon his Church, an event of grace that filled the
Upper Room in Jerusalem and then spread throughout
the world.

But what happened on that day, so distant from us
and yet so close as to touch the very depths of our hearts?
Luke gives us the answer in the passage of the Acts of the
Apostles which we have heard (2:1–11). The Evangelist
brings us back to Jerusalem, to the Upper Room where the
Apostles were gathered. The first element that draws our
attention is the sound that suddenly came from heaven
"like the rush of a violent wind," and filled the house; then
the "tongues as of fire" that divided and came to rest on
each of the Apostles. Sound and tongues of fire: these are
clear, concrete signs that touch the Apostles not only from
without but also within: deep in their minds and hearts.
As a result, "all of them were filled with the Holy Spirit,"
who unleashed his irresistible power with amazing conse-
quences: they all "began to speak in different languages,

---

1. Holy Mass with the Ecclesial Movements; May 19, 2013; St. Peter's
Square.

as the Spirit gave them ability." A completely unexpected scene opens up before our eyes: a great crowd gathers, astonished because each one heard the Apostles speaking in his own language. They all experience something new, something that had never happened before: "We hear them, each of us, speaking our own language." And what is it that they are speaking about? "God's deeds of power."

In the light of this passage from Acts, I would like to reflect on three words linked to the working of the Holy Spirit: newness, harmony, and mission.

*Newness* always makes us a bit fearful, because we feel more secure if we have everything under control, if we are the ones who build, program, and plan our lives in accordance with our own ideas, our own comfort, our own preferences. This is also the case when it comes to God. Often we follow him, we accept him, but only up to a certain point. It is hard to abandon ourselves to him with complete trust, allowing the Holy Spirit to be the soul and guide of our lives in our every decision. We fear that God may force us to strike out on new paths and leave behind our all too narrow, closed, and selfish horizons in order to become open to his own.

Yet throughout the history of salvation, whenever God reveals himself, he brings newness — God always brings newness — and demands our complete trust: Noah, mocked by all, builds an ark and is saved; Abram leaves his land with only a promise in hand; Moses stands up to the might of Pharaoh and leads his people to freedom; the Apostles, huddled fearfully in the Upper Room, go forth with courage to proclaim the Gospel.

This is not a question of novelty for novelty's sake, the search for something new to relieve our boredom, as is so often the case in our own day. The newness that God brings into our life is something that actually brings fulfillment, that gives true joy, true serenity, because God loves us and desires only our good.

Let us ask ourselves today: Are we open to "God's surprises"? Or are we closed and fearful before the newness of the Holy Spirit? Do we have the courage to strike out along the new paths that God's newness sets before us, or do we resist, barricaded in transient structures that have lost their capacity for openness to what is new? We would do well to ask ourselves these questions all through the day.

A second thought: the Holy Spirit would appear to create disorder in the Church, since he brings the diversity of charisms and gifts; yet all this, by his working, is a great source of wealth, for the Holy Spirit is the Spirit of unity, which does not mean uniformity, but which leads everything back to *harmony*. In the Church, it is the Holy Spirit who creates harmony. One of the Fathers of the Church has an expression that I love: the Holy Spirit himself is harmony — "*Ipse harmonia est.*" He is indeed harmony. Only the Spirit can awaken diversity, plurality, and multiplicity, while at the same time building unity. Here, too, when we are the ones who try to create diversity and close ourselves up in what makes us different and other, we bring division. When we are the ones who want to build unity in accordance with our human plans, we end up creating uniformity, standard-

ization. But if instead we let ourselves be guided by the
Spirit, then richness, variety, and diversity never become
a source of conflict, because he impels us to experience
variety within the communion of the Church.

Journeying together in the Church, under the guidance of her pastors, who possess a special charism and ministry, is a sign of the working of the Holy Spirit. Having a
sense of the Church is something fundamental for every
Christian, every community, and every movement. It is
the Church that brings Christ to me, and me to Christ;
parallel journeys are very dangerous! When we venture beyond (*proagon*) the Church's teaching and community —
the Apostle John tells us in his Second Letter — and do
not remain in them, we are not one with the God of Jesus
Christ (cf. 2 Jn v. 9). So let us ask ourselves: Am I open to
the harmony of the Holy Spirit, overcoming every form of
exclusivity? Do I let myself be guided by him, living in the
Church and with the Church?

A final point. The older theologians used to say
that the soul is a kind of sailboat — the Holy Spirit is
the wind that fills its sails and drives it forward, and the
gusts of wind are the gifts of the Spirit. Lacking his im-
pulse and his grace, we do not go forward. The Holy
Spirit draws us into the mystery of the living God and
saves us from the threat of a Church that is gnostic and
self-referential, closed in on herself; he impels us to open
the doors and go forth to proclaim and bear witness to
the good news of the Gospel, to communicate the joy of
faith, the encounter with Christ. The Holy Spirit is the
soul of *mission*. The events that took place in Jerusalem

almost two thousand years ago are not something far removed from us; they are events that affect us and become a lived experience in each of us.

The Pentecost of the Upper Room in Jerusalem is the beginning, a beginning that endures. The Holy Spirit is the supreme gift of the risen Christ to his Apostles, yet he wants that gift to reach everyone. As we heard in the Gospel, Jesus says: "I will ask the Father, and he will give you another Advocate to remain with you forever" (Jn 14:16). It is the Paraclete Spirit, the "Comforter," who grants us the courage to take to the streets of the world, bringing the Gospel! The Holy Spirit makes us look to the horizon and drives us to the very outskirts of existence in order to proclaim life in Jesus Christ. Let us ask ourselves: do we tend to stay closed in on ourselves, on our group, or do we let the Holy Spirit open us to mission? Today, let us remember these three words: newness, harmony, and mission.

> Today let us remember these three words: newness, harmony, and mission.

Today's liturgy is a great prayer, which the Church, in union with Jesus, raises up to the Father, asking him to renew the outpouring of the Holy Spirit. May each of us, and every group and movement, in the harmony of the Church, cry out to the Father and implore this gift. Today, too, as at her origins, the Church, in union with Mary, cries out: "*Veni, Sancte Spiritus!* Come, Holy Spirit, fill the hearts of your faithful, and kindle in them the fire of your love!" Amen.

# More Books by POPE FRANCIS
# from Our Sunday Visitor

## ONLY LOVE CAN SAVE US:
### LETTERS, HOMILIES, AND TALKS OF CARDINAL
### JORGE BERGOGLIO

## THROUGH THE YEAR WITH POPE FRANCIS:
### DAILY REFLECTIONS

Our Sunday Visitor Publishing
1-800-348-2440
www.osv.com